BUSES OF LONDON

BUSES
OF
LONDON
Colin H Curtis

An illustrated review,
with specifications and brief history,
of every London bus type
purchased by London Transport
or its predecessors
since 1908.

LONDON TRANSPORT
55 Broadway, London
SW1

© London Transport 1977
ISBN 0 85329 084 9.
Designed by William Fenton, A.R.C.A.,
set in 10pt. Times Roman
Printed in Great Britain for London Transport by
Bournehall Press Ltd., Welwyn Garden City and London

Contents

Abbreviations used in this book

THROUGHOUT THIS BOOK, the bus type codes associated with the vehicle concerned have been given, but to save space other abbreviations have been used. Some used most frequently are given below; most will be familiar to readers who already have knowledge of the world of buses but care is needed to avoid confusion (i.e. L.T. has been used when referring to London Transport, but the code L.T. was given to a six-wheeled London Bus that first appeared in 1929).

L.T. London Transport Board.
L.P.T.B. London Passenger Transport Board. (1933-1947)
L.T.B. (1963-1969)
L.T.E. London Transport Executive.
    (the above names have been used by the one monopoly transport organization in London since 1933).
L.G.O.C. } London General Omnibus Co.
General
L.G.C.S. London General Country Services.
L.C.B.S. London Country Bus Services, Ltd., associated with National Bus Company and, until 1970, the Country Area organization of London Transport.
A.E.C. Associated Equipment Co. Ltd., Southall.
P.A.Y.E. 'Pay-as-you-enter' experimental fare-collection system, later widely used in the London area.
P.R.V. Park Royal Vehicles.
E.C.W. Eastern Coachworks Ltd.

References to places in London (i.e. Plumstead, Hounslow, and so on) should be construed as applying to the London Transport Garage of that name when bus movements are under discussion. To help where there is any ambiguity, the Code reference to the garage has often been given in brackets. Reference to 'Central' should be taken as referring to the Red (Central) Bus area of London, and that to 'Country' to the old Country (Green) bus area, now the London Country Bus area.

Preface

WHEN THE IDEA of compiling 'The London Motor Bus'* was crystallised, it became necessary to undertake a good deal of research. Naturally, restrictions on space and price prevented the inclusion of everything relating to the period. This book, therefore, is intended to complement the earlier account, and forms for the first time, the complete official record of all the types of motor omnibus and coaches built or purchased new by the London General Omnibus Company Limited since its amalgamation with The London Road Car Company (Union Jack) and the Vanguard Motorbus Company in 1908 and also LONDON TRANSPORT, since its formation in 1933. Vehicles acquired from other operators have, to a large extent, been excluded except where they fill in gaps in the numbering of a specific series.

Many buses and coaches owned by the L.G.O.C. were to be found in other liveries or under different fleet names owing to certain operating agreements. These included:

EAST SURREY. Between 1921 and 1932, East Surrey Traction Company Ltd., operated a number of routes south of London with buses supplied by L.G.O.C., as well as vehicles owned by East Surrey.

NATIONAL. Between 1921 and 1932 National Omnibus & Transport Company Ltd. operated a number of routes north of London with buses and coaches supplied by the L.G.O.C.

TILLING. Between 1923 and 1933, Thomas Tilling Ltd. operated certain double- and single-deck buses in Central London on behalf of L.G.O.C. These were in addition to buses actually owned by Tilling.

East Surrey became a wholly owned subsidiary of the L.G.O.C. and operated between 1932 and 1933 under the title of LONDON GENERAL COUNTRY SERVICES LIMITED and taking over from National the operations north of London.

Although many independent companies were taken over by L.G.O.C. from 1926 to 1928, only one—Overground Ltd.—was maintained separately until 1933. Its buses are mentioned in the story.

It is hoped that this book will fulfil many functions; in particular, to record the development of the London bus in a logical manner, and to be an aid to assist model makers in the making of more permanent reminders of bygone days. Perhaps most of all it will appeal to all those who appreciate the good things of the past.

In such a work there must be mistakes and omissions, but not by design. Exhaustive searches have failed to reveal missing facts, but if it is forthcoming I shall be pleased to receive the information from readers to set the history straight.

Mention should be made of those who have generously allowed the use of photographs from their collection, including Alan B. Cross, W. J. Haynes, the late J. Higham, W. Noel Jackson, and George J. Robbins. For the efforts of George Robbins who gave great assistance in the provision of much information, as well as advice in the creation of this book, and to the Publicity Officer and his staff for technical help, I am indeed grateful.

COLIN CURTIS 1977

* The London Motor Bus, by J. Graeme Bruce & Colin Curtis, is published by London Transport at £3.50.
A complete history of East Surrey Traction Company Ltd., from 1911 to 1932 will be found in EAST SURREY by 'Bell Street' (H. J. Publications, St. Albans. 1975. Price £2.50)

1 X Type 1909

THE X TYPE VEHICLE could be claimed to be the first of the vehicles to be built primarily for London and was the forerunner of this policy which continued to include the introduction of the Routemaster in 1959.

The design was created in 1909 at the old Vanguard Works at Walthamstow one year after the amalgamation of the General, Road Car, and Vanguard Fleets. Admittedly the 'X' was a combination of the best of all the vehicles operating at the time but it incorporated a good deal of the Daimler, Wolseley and Straker Squire types. The 'X' should really be considered as the prototype for the famous 'B' type which was to emerge the following year.

Sixty buses and one lorry were built in 1909–10. For most of their existence they operated from Middle Row (X). All were withdrawn early in 1914 but 46 were re-licensed in 1915 and finally withdrawn in 1920.

They employed a 28 hp engine with a cone clutch. Seating was 16 inside and 18 outside.

(*Below*) X type bus loading a Sunday School 'treat'. Note driver heavily protected from the weather. The open transmission to the rear wheels is clearly shown.

2 B Type 1910

THE FIRST B type employed a similar engine to the X type, but by increasing the bore and ultimately the stroke, a 40 HP engine was created for later vehicles. In conjunction with the more powerful engine, the cone clutch gave way to the single-plate Ferodo.

B1 entered service on 18 October 1910 on route 25 and during the next three years 2678 were built; most running as buses in London. The bonnet number was also the chassis number and several were in use as vans or lorries. Following the formation of A.E.C. in 1912 some B type vehicles were sold to other operators. In 1912 eighteen B types were adapted as sixteen seat single-deckers for operating the Blackwall Tunnel service.

Other variations at the time were:

55 double-deck were operated in the red livery of Associated Omnibus Co.

100 double-deck were operated in the green livery of the Metropolitan Steam Omnibus Company.

124 double-deck were operated in the blue livery of Tramways (M.E.T.) Omnibus Company. In addition to 226 Daimlers which were commandeered by the Government in 1914.

10 double-deck operated in the blue livery of Southern (South Metropolitan Electric Tramways).

12 double-deck operated in the blue livery of Central (London Central Omnibus Company who also ran a number of Leylands.)

Production restarted in early 1914 at B2679 and continued until the build ceased at 2826 owing to the war. Over 1000 B type were commandeered for War Service in 1914/15 and a number went overseas to the front line. Many returned to London service after the war, including B43, now to be seen in the Imperial War Museum.

In 1919, 250 new B vehicles (type 7), B4879–5132, were built and allocated to Cricklewood and Willesden garages.

Notable variations:

B1000 double-deck with luxury body for Private Hire.

B1354 and 1357. Fitted with open char-a-banc body.

B1394 fitted with (1) second hand single-deck Private Hire body with front and rear entrance.
(2) Prototype 20-seat single-deck bentwood body with forward facing seats.

B1425 Experimental double-deck with forward facing seats.

B1499 fitted with second-hand double-deck private hire body.

B1858 & 1873 Prototype bentwood double-deck 32 seaters with forward facing seats. Twenty were eventually built.

B2679–2708 thirty single-deck with 20 seat bentwood bodies, all went to the War Department in 1914 as ambulances.

B3474–3503 Further delivery of 20 seat single-deck.

B4879–4878 Ten new chassis fitted with cut down double-deck bodies to make sixteen seat single-deck for munition services in 1917.

B6865–6889 Fifteen replacement buses for Tramways (M.E.T.) and ten for Gearless Omnibus Co.

B4900 A former double-deck was the prototype for a new and improved type of single-deck seating 26, similar to the K type, 75 were later built mainly from the B4900–5132 batch. Some were later altered to 20 seaters for Muswell Hill routes.

B533 Converted to producer gas in 1918, twenty were approved but no more converted.

In 1922 ten B type were fitted with Daimler engines, pneumatic tyres and K type gearbox. Eight were mounted with 19-seat char-a-banc bodies and renumbered C1–4/7–10, seven being used by National. B1064 (C4) was retained by L.G.O.C. for private hire. C5/6 were small one-man buses operated by National.

The last double-deck B type in passenger service was withdrawn in 1926; the last single-deck in 1927. B340 is in the London Transport Collection.

A more comprehensive account of the B type is given in 'The London B type Motor Omnibus' by G. J. Robbins and J. B. Atkinson.

Chassis details

Track	5′ 8″
Overall length	19′ 2¼″ Double-Deck, 23′ 2⅝″ & 24′ 0⅛″ Single-Deck
Wheelbase	12′ 10⅝″ Double-Deck, 14′ 6″ Single-Deck
Frame	Ash with steel plates
Front axle	Straight H-Section (28 hp engine), shaped H-Section (40 hp engine)
Rear axle	7⅓ Reduction worm
Gearbox	3 speed forward chain gear; spur reverse
Clutch	28/30 hp leather cone; 40 hp Ferodo single plate
Engine*	28 hp: 110 mm bore × 140 mm stroke; 40 hp: 115 mm bore × 140 mm stroke
Suspension	Leaf springs
Brakes	Drum with internal expanding shoes transmission handbrake (sprag gear for hilly routes)

* Official records show a 3rd type of engine—AEC type 5 with 120 mm bore×150 mm stroke
On the basis of RAC hp the values become

110 mm = 29·8 hp	AEC type 3 engine
115 mm = 32·7 hp	Presumably AEC 4
120 mm = 35·8 hp	AEC type 5 engine

Body details (Double-Deck)

Overall height	12′ 5″	*Overall width*	6′ 11″
Seating, inside	16	*Seating, outside*	18
Unladen weight	4 tons	*Laden weight*	6 tons 2 cwts 2 qts
Angle of tilt	29°		

Single-Deck seating capacities varied from 16–26 seats

(*Left*) B type, No. 2384 undergoing tilt-test at Chiswick, probably about 1911. The early photographer obviously had problems with this remarkable indoor shot. The length of exposure can be deduced from the 'ghosts' of two figures affecting the time exposure.

(*Above*) B 1064, after fitment of pneumatic tyres and charabanc body. The retractable hood worked backwards to cover the whole or part of the rear of the bus, leaving the driver always exposed. Note the high step. This shot was taken outside Theobalds Park, Cheshunt.

(*Below*) B type charabanc, showing leather hood retaining straps, outside North Road Coach works. This was one of six charabancs new in the summer of 1914.

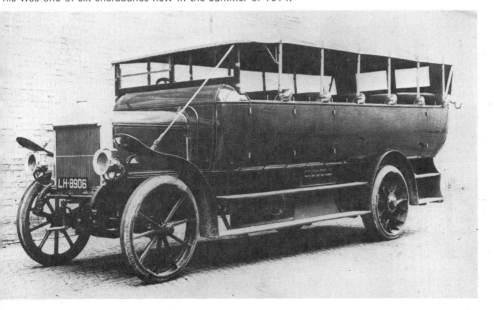

(*Above*) B type fitted with a device to prevent overrunning pedestrians. In those days tram passengers were forced to move into the centre of the road to board, and ran the risk of accident from buses approaching the kerb.

(*Top right*) Conventional B type of post-war days. The slatted side panels were fitted to all London buses and designed to be easily sawn through to recover pedestrians trapped beneath. Route boards and livery show style in use since 1920.

(*Bottom right*) This late-mark B type was originally double-deck, but has been converted here to a 26-seater single deck bus. It is shown here outside Camden Villas and little care has been taken to see that authentic route plates are carried—there are plates for Route 41 and 80a, and the blinds applied to the 111 services.

PRIVATE·MOTOR·OMNIBUSES·FOR·HIRE.

B.1394

B1394

FOR TERMS APPLY TO L.G.O.C.
PRIVATE HIRE DEPT. 9 GROSVENOR RD. S.W.

(*Above*) Publicity postcard for Private Hire. The time is about 1911. This photograph should be compared with the following one; the same bus is involved, but here the chassis has a rear-loading straight-sided body with upholstered seating.

(*Below*) B1394 with bus body accommodating 20 seats. It is photographed working the Route 79 (Kingston to Esher) at Long Ditton. The body is the prototype of the bentwood style.

KINGSTON MARKET, PORTSMOUTH-RD. ESHER, HIGH-ST
GENERAL

3 K Type 1919

THE K TYPE was the forerunner of the modern bus. By incorporating wheel arches at the rear it was possible to design the body to the full width permitted by the current regulations. With the driver alongside the engine (forward control) instead of behind it (normal control) greater capacity was available for passengers—46 instead of 34 passenger in earlier types. The engine utilised for the K was the lower powered B type.

K 1 and 2 were in service by September 1919, and 1060 double-deck buses were in use by September 1921. Another fifteen were added in 1924 and 55 more in 1925/26 bringing the maximum total to 1132. K 1078–1101, a batch of twenty-four single-deckers, seating 24, were the first General buses to be fitted with pneumatic tyres. In 1926 twenty double-deckers were fitted with new 22-seat single-deck bodies and were painted silver grey for

Below) Open-top K type, photographed about 1925.

the Morden extension of the City & South London Railway (later the Northern Line).
A further 84 double-deck buses were converted to single-deckers with new 20 or 24 seat
bodies. Many retained their solid tyres and were fitted with sprag gear for use on hilly
routes. Finally, in 1927, eleven double-deck buses were fitted with 30-seat single-deck
bodies after the chassis were lengthened.

In 1923 a few buses were fitted with an experimental 16″ windscreen on the top deck
but they were soon withdrawn. Thirty double-deckers were on loan to East Surrey
between 1923 and 1930 in addition to twelve they owned. A number of single-deck
buses were also loaned to both National and Easy Surrey. Several double-decker buses
ran in the liveries of acquired Independents in 1926/27.

In 1926 about 100 double-deck bodies were rebuilt with longitudinal seating for the
lower deck which reduced the total capacity to 44, compared to the normal standard o
46 with buses fitted with transverse seating.

Double-deck K type were all withdrawn from service by early 1931 except for ten which
were retained for route 90 owing to a weight restriction on Chertsey Bridge. This con
tinued until June 1932 when they were finally withdrawn. The single-deckers were also
withdrawn in 1931. K 424 is in the London Transport Collection.

Chassis details MAKER'S REF: AEC MODEL 3 CHASSIS TYPE 301/2/3/4/5

Track	5′ 10″ Double-Deck, 5′ 11″ Single-Deck
Overall length	22′ 7⅝″ (30 seater Single 26′ 0″, others 22′ 5¾″)
Wheelbase	14′ 2¼″. See Notes
Frame	Ash with 5/32″ Steel Plate. Max. width 3′ 6½″
Front Axle	Plain Bearings, width over hub caps 6′ 9½″
Rear Axle	Worm gear 8¼:1 reduction width over hub caps 7′ 0¼″, certain single-deckers 6·3/5:1
Gearbox	3 speed chain gear. Spur reverse
Clutch	Dry multiplate steel/Ferodo (Double-Decker). Hele-Shaw multiplate in oil (Single-Deckers)
Engine	28 HP 100 mm. bore × 140 mm. stroke
Suspension	Semi elliptical leaf springs
Brakes	Drum with internal expanding shoes
Turning/Circle	60′

Body details (Double-Deck)

Overall height	12′ 2″	*Overall width*	7′ 1″
Seating inside	22	*Seating outside*	24
Angle of tilt	30½°		
Unladen weight	3 tons 17 cwt	*Laden weight*	6 tons 15 cwt

LGOC CONVERSIONS (*other than* 30 SEATER *Single-Deck*)

Overall height	8′ 7″	*Overall width*	7′ 0″
Unladen weight	3 tons 10 cwt	*Laden weight*	5 tons 0 cwt

30 SEATER

Overall height	9′ 2¼″	*Overall width*	7′ 0″
Unladen weight	4 tons 5 cwt	*Laden weight*	6 tons 8 cwt

Vehicles built
1132 Double-Deck, 24 Single-Deck
From the Double-Decks (a) 20 were converted to 22 seat Single-Deck
(b) 84 were converted to 20 or 24 seat Single-Deck
(c) 11 were converted to 30 seat Single-Deck
with 16′ 7½″ wheel base

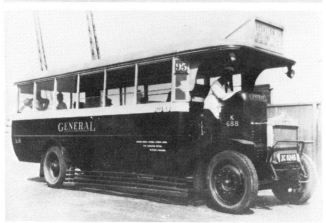

(*Above*) Single-deck K type bus. This vehicle was one of 20 special vehicles that ran as 'feeders' to the Morden Underground extensions. The photograph shows the vehicle during the time that these special buses were painted in the distinctive silver livery.

(*Centre*) The first single-deck K type bus. Operating from Hounslow garage, it worked the Burnham Beeches to Leatherhead service, which became Route 462 after the formation of the London Transport organization in 1933. The detailed and rather fussy lining of the bodywork caused difficulty with maintenance.

(*Below*) K 688, a 30-seater, in the later livery of deep maroon and yellow, a combination of colours adapted for convenience of maintenance which gave rise to the nickname of 'rhubarb and custard' amongst the bus crews at Hounslow Garage.

W. Noel Jackson

4 S Type 1920

WHEN THE MAXIMUM weight allowance for a double-decker was increased to 8 tons it allowed a development of the K type to be produced, which was known as the S type. The seating capacity was raised to 54 passengers and the engine size increased slightly giving a 35 hp rating. The S type was the first to have larger wheels and also larger route number stencils back and front and in the centre of the side windows. The latter practice was discontinued after December 1924.

The first fifteen S type were in service by January 1921 and 895 S type buses were in use in London by September 1923. Sixty-four of them were 30-seat single-deck and these included fourteen for National. S 896 was at first a 30-seat charabanc with bucket-type seats and a folding hood so that it was referred to as an all-weather coach, but it was later converted to a double-deck bus. S 897–90, 902–914 were later additions to the double-deck fleet. S 901 was a standard single-deck for National whilst S 915–27, new in 1927, were also National single-deckers with improved 30-seat bodies to the same style as the K type single-deckers. They also had pneumatic tyres. S 928 was at first a ticket van, but this vehicle subsequently metamorphozed into a double-deck bus.

All the General and National single-deck S types were converted to use pneumatic tyres in 1928.

The double-deck S type was withdrawn in 1931, but many of the single-deckers continued in service until taken over by London Transport, being finally withdrawn in 1935. Before this, they had been fitted with windscreens to the driver's cab.

The 502 design was an adaption of the S type but to a heavier class of vehicle designed for Provincial service, and the L.G.O.C. purchased fifty for use by National and East

Surrey. In the former fleet they were given bonnet numbers PS 1 to PS 15 and they had the standard type of double-deck S body. The East Surrey, however, had a new design of body with an NS-style canopy over the driver's cab. They were built by Ransomes. Eight more of the later 507 type were added to the East Surrey fleet in 1927. All PS East Surrey buses had 48-seat bodies, whilst National had 43 seats at first, and 54 later.

Most were withdrawn in 1931, but twelve of the East Surrey vehicles survived to London Transport days for use on the 410 route until replaced by the 'Godstone' STLs in 1934.

Chassis details MAKER'S REF: A.E.C. MODEL 4 CHASSIS 401-L.G.O.C., 403 AND 502/507 PROVINCIAL

Track	Front 6′ 0½″, rear 5′ 10″
Overall length	24′ 8¼″ *Wheelbase* 14′ 11″
Frame	Ash with $\frac{5}{32}$″ plates, max. width 3′ 6½″
Front axle	I Section. Roller bearings. Width over hub caps 7′ 0¾″
Rear axle	Worm gear 9¼:1. Width over hub caps 7′ 0¼″
Gearbox	3 speed chain gear spur reverse
Clutch	Single plate dry steel/Ferodo
Engine	35 hp 108 mm. bore × 140 mm. stroke
Suspension	Semi-elliptical leaf assisted by compound volute
Brakes	Expanding Ferodo linings acting on pressed steel drums
Steering	Worm-and-nut

(*Left*) An S bus on Private Hire work. The time is 1923. The smaller advertisements carried on the saloon casement windows were transparencies, tending to give the interior something of the atmosphere of a Victorian church on sunny days.

(*Below*) S371 waits at Windsor Castle hill as the driver scurries off for some well-earned refreshment. This single-decker from Uxbridge garage is working the 503 route which the L.G.O.C. took over from Thames Valley Traction Company in 1929.   *J. Higham*

Body details

Overall height	12' 4½"	*Unladen weight*	
Overall width	7' 1"	Double-Deck 4 tons 10 cwt.	
Seating (Double-Deck)		Single-Deck 4 tons 5 cwt.	
inside 26, outside 28		*Laden weight*	
Angle of tilt 29°		Double-Deck 8 tons 10 cwt.	
Single-Deck, 30 seater		Single-Deck 6 tons 10 cwt.	

Vehicles built (originally)

DOUBLE-DECK	SINGLE-DECK
849	79* S type
50	— PS (502 type)
8	— PS (507 type)

* includes 28 for National

(*Top right*) S type charabanc engaged on Private Hire work. About 1924.

(*Below*) S822, a single-decker running from Athol Street garage on the Blackwall Tunnel service. Compare this with the earlier picture showing an S type bus with heavy pneumatic tyres.

(*Centre right*) S type bus in Kenton Road, near Kenton Station. This route was afterwards worked with lowbridge ST type buses. *J. Higham*

(*Bottom right*) A National S type in L.G.C.S. livery, operated by the L.G.O.C. The body is an adaptation from the 'K' type; compare with illustration below (page 14). There are no garage codes carried —the country bus side of London Transport did not adopt the coding system until 1935. This scene dates from about 1932 and shows the bus near the Ridgeway. *J. Higham*

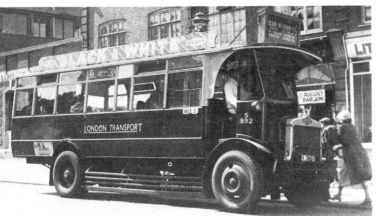

5 NS Type 1923

ALTHOUGH A CONTINUATION of the S type, the NS had many advantages. It employed a dropped frame so that the high platform at the rear was avoided and a lower centre of gravity was achieved. Although NS 1 was designed with a covered top deck, this was not allowed by the Metropolitan Police at that time and when the NS type eventually entered service in London in May 1923, they all had the familiar open-top deck. During the next two years 1747 were built and operated to the same style. Thirty-one were sent to National and 27 to East Surrey. The Surrey based company also purchased eight other NS for their own use which were not numbered in the NS series.

Four buses with covered top deck (NS 1734–37) were built and put into service in London in October 1925 as an experiment. This was successful and passed by the police so the L.G.O.C. were permitted to build more of this type. Therefore, a further 580 NS were built with covered tops and top covers were fitted to 1684 of the earlier bodies.

In June 1928, following an increase in the permitted width of London buses, pneumatic tyres were fitted to the NS type using giant tyres on the rear wheels. The first of these were fifty of the ADC 422 (NS 2297–2346). These had a wider body and improved seating. Eventually pneumatic tyres and windscreens to the drivers' cabs were fitted to most of the type.

An interesting adaptation of the type were the twenty-five buses built with a special body for working through Blackwall Tunnel. The top deck was narrow with dropped gangways and back to back seating, the lower deck had longitudinal seating. They had

(*Below*) An early NS bus at Chiswick Works. The front seat, to the side of the driver, was provided for special officials in possession of riding passes—usually inspectors from the Public Carriage Office, Traffic controllers, and some District Superintendents.

enclosed staircases and the seating capacity was 46. The prototype was NS 2050, the others being between NS 2210 and 2229. All retained their solid tyres, with the exception of NS 2213, which was fitted with pneumatics at a later date as an experiment. Six further tunnel-type buses with more normal seating and open staircases were later built and mounted on earlier chassis.

Two L.G.O.C. buses (NS 1760 and 2015) and one East Surrey (NS 1758) were fitted temporarily with six-cylinder engines and the seating capacity reduced to 44.

The final order for twenty-five NS (2347–2371) was cancelled and diverted to other operators, but in 1929 six more NS (2372–77) were added to the fleet. NS 2378 was a demonstration vehicle added to the East Surrey fleet.

NS 1738 was an experimental single-deck version of NS, known as DNS. It had a semi-saloon body seating 30 and used for private hire.

In 1933 London Transport acquired thirty-three NS from 'British' and these were given numbers NS 2379–2411. They retained their solid tyres and were soon withdrawn.

The last NS type bus ran in 1937, but several were pressed into service as Staff Canteens and other ancillary vehicles.

NS 1995 has been preserved in the London Transport Collection.

Chassis details MAKER'S REF: A.E.C. MODEL 4 CHASSIS 405, 407, 408, 409, 410 and 422

Track	Front 6′ 0½″, rear 5′ 9¾″ solid tyres
	Front 6′ 2½″, rear 6′ 0⅝″ pneumatic
Overall length	26′ 0″
Wheelbase	15′ 6″
Frame	Pressed steel 8 mm. thick
Front axle	I Section. Bar. Roller bearings. Width over hub caps 7′ 0⅝″ solid, 7′ 5″ pneumatic
Rear axle	Roller bearing hubs, 10·21 worm, 19·84 spur. Worm-and-spur gear 9·28:1 double reduction. Width over hub caps 7′ 1⅜″ solid, 7′ 4⅞″ pneumatic
Gearbox	3 speed chain gear
Clutch	Heleshaw multiplate running in oil.
Engine	35 hp 108 mm. bore × 140 mm. stroke 4 cyl.
Suspension	Leaf springs
Turning circle	60′ 0″

Body details

OPEN TOP

Overall height 11′ 8″	*Overall width* 7′ 2″
Seating inside 24	*Seating outside* 26/28
Unladen weight 5 tons 17 cwt.	*Laden weight* 9 tons 6 cwt.

COVERED TOP

Overall height 14′ 3″	*Overall width* 7′ 2″
Seating inside 24	*Seating outside* 28
Unladen weight 6 tons 5 cwt.	*Laden weight* 9 tons 11 cwt.

Angle of tilt 28° (solid tyres with top deck load)

Vehicles built (originally)

1748 Double-Deck open top including 31 for National and 27 for East Surrey
580 Covered top
56 ADC 422 covered top, plus demonstration bus for East Surrey
Included in these figures are two batches of tunnel buses of 25 and 6, these latter 6 being fitted on earlier chassis. Retrospective fitment of tops to earlier open top buses (1684 in total).
A Single-Deck version of NS known as DNS existed but only one was built—a coach seating 30—bonnet No. NS 1738.

(*Above*) NS 170, showing rear entrance.

(*Below*) The first NS covered-top bus. This vehicle never entered service in the form shown; it failed to get approval from the police. Note the curious mixture of route numbers and destinations.

18

(*Above*) Later NS. bus. The police finally approved a total of four buses as an experimental service. The route which ran from Elephant & Castle to Epping (Route 100) was selected as it represented a cross-section of every type of London street, including tram overhead obstructions, as well as the more obvious problems with overhanging trees in the Country Bus area.

(*Below*) NS 1738, also known as the DNS. An experimental Reliance vehicle.

(*Left*) Blackwall Tunnel bus—NS 2050. The year is 1927. The enamelled-iron plate at the rear of the bus is the Metropolitan Stage Carriage number, carried on all London's buses, trams and taxis. The number was carried at both ends of trams and on the rear platform as well as the rear on buses.

(*Right*) NS 2050. Front view. The upper saloon was fitted with back-to-back bucket seats to assist fare collection.

(*Below*) NS in its final form, about 1935.

6 DE Type* and ADC 419 1926

IN JUNE 1926 eight coaches of a new pattern were added to the L.G.O.C. private hire fleet. They carried 24-seat all metal open coach bodies with folding hoods, built at Chiswick. The seating arrangement was four pairs of seats on each side of a central gangway with two seats over each wheel arch facing inwards. At the rear there were four seats across the full width of the body. The chassis was considered as an NS with a Daimler engine. Except for a few minor differences, including a three-speed gearbox, their specification was identical with the standard 419 type.

The L.G.O.C. purchased 33 of the 419s in 1927 for their private hire fleet and these had similar 28-seat open coach bodies with folding hoods which led them to be designated 'All Weather Coaches'. Together with the earlier eight they were allotted fleet numbers AW 1 to AW 41, but these numbers were not displayed on the vehicles. In the main they served as private hire coaches but were often used as spares on Green Line services. Four were allocated to National.

The East Surrey had six 419s in 1927; these later became the property of Green Line.

AW 1–8 were sold in 1929 but the other 33 were re-built in 1930 with 28-seat Short Bros., semi-saloon coach bodies. All were withdrawn and sold by 1933.

* Daimler experimental

Chassis details MAKER'S REF: DAIMLER EXPTL

Rear axle	9·244:1 ratio
Gearbox	3 speed K type/4 speed also
Engine	Daimler sleeve valve, 97 mm. bore × 130 mm. stroke

Body details

Seating 24(DE) 28(ADC)   *Unladen weight* 4 tons 13 cwt.

Vehicles built

AW1–41: comprising 8 DE, 33, 419 private hire fleet, 6, 419 Easy Surrey (not numbered)
The 419 employed a 6-cyl. Daimler sleeve-valve engine of 81·5 mm. stroke and 140 mm. stroke with a single plate clutch, with a 4 speed gearbox. The wheelbase was 15′ 8″

(*Below*) DE Private Hire Coach. The development of the folding hood is shown here—the cover could be extended forwards to shield the whole of the coach, including the driver, from the effects of a teasing shower or strong winds.

7 LS Type 1927

ALTHOUGH THESE MASSIVE six-wheeled vehicles were grouped into the one class, known as the LS or 'London Six', they nearly all differed in various ways. The first two were built with inside staircases similar to the style of the NS 'tunnel' buses. LS3 had an open staircase, and LS1 and 2 were quickly converted. Seating varied from 64 to 70 or 72 passengers, but all were ultimately reduced to 56 seats.

The LS was the first double-deck bus fitted with pneumatic tyres as the twin rear wheels did not need the giant tyres of the NS and so did not exceed the width restriction at that time.

The chassis were produced by the Associated Daimler organization which for a time was a joint venture by Associated Equipment Company and Daimler Motor Co. Originally the Daimler sleeve-valve engine was used but later the AEC 108 mm. bore × 140 mm. stroke engine was fitted.

LS 6 was a single-deck seating 34 and for a time had petrol-electric transmission. It spent its life at Cricklewood garage working on route 104 (later numbered 240).

LS 1 entered service on route 16 in June 1927 aod LS 2 followed a few months later. Others ran on routes 29 and 33, but eventually all were concentrated at Cricklewood for route 16.

Although withdrawn from service in 1937 four (LS 3, 6, 8 and 10) were converted to heavy breakdown tenders and continued as such until 1951. LS 1 became a temporary waiting room at Sevenoaks!

Chassis details MAKER'S REF: A.E.C. MODEL 8 CHASSIS 802

Track	Front 5' 11", rear 6' 0¾"
Overall length	29' 8¼"
Wheelbase	18' 10½" (rear bogie)
Frame	Pressed steel channel, max. width 4' 11"
Front axle	I section stamping roller bearings, width over hub caps 7' 4¼"
Rear axle	Worm gear 8¼:1, width over wheel studs 7' 2"
Gearbox	4 speed spur
Clutch	Single plate, dry
Engine	A.E.C. 6-cyl. overhead cam, 108 mm. bore× 140 mm. stroke, 48 hp at 1000 rpm or Daimler sleeve, 97 mm. bore × 130 mm. stroke
Suspension	2 leaf springs front, 4 leaf springs rear
Turning circle	64' 0"

Body details (Double-Deck)

Overall height 14' 3¼" front unladen   *Unladen weight* 7 tons 7 cwt (66 seat version)
(rear, unladen 14' 5¾", laden 14' 3")   *Laden weight* 12 tons 7 cwt (55 seat version)
Overall width 7' 2"
Seating   LS1: 66   LS3, 4, 5, 8, 9, 10, 11: 70
            LS2: 64

Vehicles built

11 Double-Deck, 1 Single-Deck LS6: 34 seater

(*Above*) One of 12 LS buses. This has a closed staircase, which gave rise to difficulties with blind changing.
They were too heavy and too slow (all London buses of the time were restricted to 12 m.p.h., but these machines were ponderous).

(*Left*) LS 9, with open staircase, as built.

(*Below*) LS 6, the only single-decker.

EARLY IN 1928 the L.G.O.C. purchased fourteen 416A type for private hire. Four were allocated to National. They had 28-seat coach bodies. At the same time thirty-nine 416s were purchased for National and fitted with 30-seat single-deck bus bodies.

During 1927/28 twenty-five 416A type had been added to the East Surrey fleet, having 30-seat single-deck bus bodies. Fourteen of these were the property of the East Surrey, who also had five 416D buses.

The L.G.O.C. supplied one other 416 type to East Surrey and this had a 46-seat all-metal lightweight double-deck body. As it was shortly afterwards equipped with a Reliance' engine, it was afterwards classed as of that type.

In 1930 the fourteen private-hire coach bodies were replaced by the bus bodies from the Reliances and added to the National fleet and they then had a total of 53 416s which were numbered AD 1–53.

Two small coaches of the 427 type were obtained in 1928 and fitted with 18-seat saloon bodies. They were used for private hire, later transferred to National, and numbered AD 54/5 to run as buses in various centres in the Country bus area. All the AD vehicles were withdrawn in 1935.

Based on an extended ADC 423 chassis, a luxurious twenty-seat body was built to make a personal 'parlour coach' for the then Chairman, Lord Ashfield. It was numbered PR1 and was fitted with full refreshment facilities.

Below) This photograph shows a Country Bus area ADC 416A bus, with a PS body. It was first owned by the East Surrey Traction Company. It was the first bus with a driver's door. Notice the apron, neatly rolled, which protected the driver from bad weather. Route 21, on which the bus is running, was a local route from South Merstham to Reigate (South Park). *J. Higham*

Chassis details (416) MAKER'S REF: A.E.C. MODEL 4 CHASSIS 416

Track	Front 5' 7", rear 5' 5¾"
Overall length	25' 7½"
Wheelbase	16' 0"
Frame	Pressed steel channel
Front axle	I section, taper roller bearings
Rear axle	Worm gear 8¼:1, taper roller bearings
Gearbox	4 speed spur
Clutch	Daimler single plate dry Ferodo
Engine	AEC 4-cylinder (416), 108 mm. bore × 140 mm. stroke
	or Daimler 6-cylinder (419), 81·5 mm. bore × 114 mm. stroke
Suspension	Leaf springs with auxiliary leaves at rear
Brakes	4 wheel internal expanding shoes
Turning circle	60' 0"
Steering	Worm-and-nut

Body details (416)

Overall height	7' 9⅝"	*Overall width*	7' 5"
Seating	28		
Unladen weight	5 tons 9 cwt.	*Laden weight*	7 tons 12 cwt.
Unladen weight (417)	5 tons 2 cwt.	*Laden weight* (417)	6 tons 11 cwt.
Unladen weight (419)	4 tons 13 cwt.	*Laden weight* (419)	6 tons 13 cwt.

Vehicles built

14 416a including 4 for East Surrey. Private hire 28 seats
39 416 for National. Private hire 30 seats
25 416a including 14 for East Surrey. Private hire 30 seats
 5 416a for East Surrey
 1 416 Double–Deck for East Surrey. Private hire 46 seats
 1 423 Parlour coach

(*Below*) A normal control ADC in Grays High Street. This is a rare photograph from the early days of London Transport (the bus is still painted in 'General' livery). The route ran for only a short time, along Grays High Street to a turning point beyond a level crossing at the 'King's Arms'. Delays were inevitable and route alterations were made in Grays to avoid the problem. The bus ran from the first garage at Grays—in Brewery Yard off Argent Street.   *J. Higham*

(*Top right*) Lord Ashfield's Parlour Coach—PR1.

(*Centre right*) ADC 419, provided with sliding roof for Private Hire work. The inadequate display board could be turned to allow the bus to run on Green Line services. The vehicle ran from Brixton Hill Private Hire Garage, from which the first of London's Green Line services (Charing X to Watford, and Golders Green to Watford) were to run. The depot was closed shortly before the second World War.

(*Bottom right*) An ADC 416 coach at Chiswick Works.

9 **R Type** 1928

INTRODUCED in 1928, this vehicle could be considered as the forerunner of the later 'T' class. With servo-assisted four-wheel brakes and a six-cylinder petrol engine it represented a great advance on earlier models. The L.G.O.C. purchased twenty of these vehicles in May 1929 with 32-seat semi-saloon coach bodies for Private Hire and they were used later for Green Line services. A month later fourteen Reliances with 29-seat saloon bus bodies were obtained for National.

Early in 1930, five more Reliances were obtained and fitted with the 28-seat coach bodies of the 416 type. Nine of the National Reliances were given the other coach bodies, leaving five Reliance buses still in the National fleet. These changes resulted in 34 coaches being used for Private Hire and also for Green Line. They were numbered R1–34. The National buses were afterwards numbered R45–R49.

Nine further Reliances were acquired by London Transport late in 1933 from Batten Coaches and they were numbered R35–43. In 1935 four of the Reliance coaches were sold and the remainder were fitted with new Weymann 30-seat all-metal bus bodies. They were painted green for use in the Country Area. The former East Surrey double deck Reliance was fitted with one of these Weymann bodies and numbered R44.

Three years later the Reliance chassis were sold and the Weymann bus bodies transferred to the T type stock, with the designation 11T11.

Chassis details MAKER'S REF: RELIANCE CHASSIS 660

Track	6′ 1 3/16″ front, 5′ 9¾″ rear
Overall length	25′ 8¾″
Frame	Pressed steel channel
Rear axle	Worm gear 6¼:1 or 5½:1 bevel
Gearbox	4 speed spur gear
Clutch	Inverted cone
Engine	6-cylinder 95 bhp. petrol, 100 mm. bore × 130 mm. stroke
Suspension:	Leaf springs
Brakes	4 wheel servo-assisted
Turning circle	60′ 0″

Body details

Overall height	8′ 5¾″
Overall width	7′ 4″
Seating	32

Unladen weight 5 tons 14 cwt.
Laden weight 8 tons 0 cwt.

Vehicles built

0 semi-saloon body, 32 seater
4 saloon body for National, 29 seater
5 coach body from 416 type, 28 seater
Also 9 acquired from Battens Coaches R35–43
935 30 rebodied by Weymann
937 body fitted to 'T' type chassis

Left) A.E.C. Reliance coach at Gerrards Cross about 1928. This was the first of the luxury Private
Hire Coaches, and the predecessors of the 'T' type. The chassis were later rebodied to become the 'R'
type.

Below) 'R' type, after fitment of new Weymann body. After refurbishing, the buses were later
transferred to work in the Country Bus area. However, they always ran as buses, and the small 'B'
symbol beside the type code on the bonnet was a device used only by the Country Bus area staff to
mark a vehicle committed to bus work. The more modern appearance to that of the first 'T' type bus
bodies arose because the conversions were carried out some time after the appearance of the 'T' type.

10 T Type (Petrol) 1929

FOR SOME REASON the 'T' class label was used to group many of the single-deck fleet of London's buses and coaches, whether petrol engined or diesel. In this way, the 'T' class could lay claim to be the longest running class in service. In AEC 'language' they were all based on the Regal chassis type 662, or, if oil-engined, 0662. (see also Chapter 23)

The first vehicles in the class were fifty rear-entrance 30-seat buses bought new in 1929. These were T1–37/39–50, 156. Five were transferred to East Surrey in 1931 and they eventually passed to the Country Department of London Transport and always retained their rear entrances. The remainder were re-built to front entrance between 1933–35. T43 was fitted experimentally with an AEC 8-cylinder engine. In 1950 twenty-six were fitted with oil engines from scrapped STL vehicles after eighteen had refurbished bodies by Marshalls of Cambridge fitted to extend their life.

T38 was fitted with a 28-seat saloon coach body for express coach operation, which led to the development of Green Line services. For this purpose 150 T-type coaches were ordered and delivered in 1930. These had 27-seat rear-entrance coach bodies and at first were operated in General, East Surrey and Autocar livery, but all were transferred to Green Line after its formation in July 1930. These coaches were numbered T51–149, 155/157–206. All were withdrawn as coaches in 1938.

T150–4, used on Private Hire, had 32-seat all-weather bodies with canvas hoods.

T207–306 were further coaches for Green Line having 30-seat front-entrance bodies. Three of these were fitted with the early AEC oil engines of 110 mm. bore and 142 stroke from new which was later exchanged for the 8·8 litre 6-cylinder oil engine. They had the distinction of operating from the AEC works at Southall on the Oxford Circus–Uxbridge Green Line service.

In 1938 twenty-six of these coaches were fitted with the Weymann all-metal bodies from the R class and given new six-cylinder 7·7 litre oil engines. The other five Weymann bodies were put on to later members of the T class. All 31 were re-coded 11T11.

The numbers T307–318 were allocated to vehicles operated by Thomas Tilling but owned by L.G.O.C. They were allocated to Bromley and ran on service 109 (later 227). For a time the first two were fitted with Daimler pre-selective gearbox. Minor changes had been made to the braking whereby hydraulic servo systems were fitted against the earlier servo only, making the chassis code 3T.

(*Below*) T26, at the rear of Hertford Garage, c. 1929. This was one of five transferred to East Surrey in 1931 and which retained the rear entrance. This fine old bus ran for many years on Route 350.

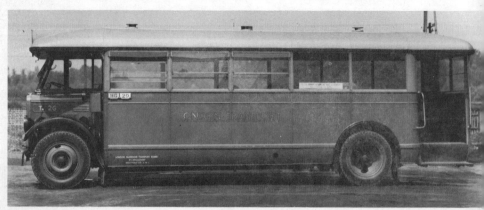

Green Line worked a number of coaches it had acquired or were on hire to it
and for operating purposes it gave them numbers T307–358. These included twenty-
one Autocar coaches (T325–345) which were passed to Maidstone & District Motor
Services in 1933 and not to London Transport. In 1935 the overlapping numbers T307–
318 were changed to T391–402. The intervening numbers T359–390, were allocated
to East Surrey and other buses acquired by London Transport in 1933/34. A few T type
were converted to producer gas operation during the second World War. T class buses
lasted until 1950; the rebuilt buses and the 11T11s until 1953. T219, in 1950, was repainted
in the original Green Line livery and is now in the London Transport Collection.

Above) A 'T' type in General 'Central' livery, with plates for Nunhead Garage. It ran on Route 621
—the Peckham–Nunhead Circular service now P3.

Below) T155 a 'T' type petrol-engined coach with a Chiswick-built body, a rare glimpse of a
vehicle in the transient livery of light red. This was the first 'T' type to be used as an Express Coach;
note the painted display destinations on the louvres. It ran from March 1930 (from the old Slough
Garage at Alpha Street) on the London–Windsor service. Trouble arose when the passengers for red
bus 81 boarded in error as the minimum fare was 3d (about 1p). The coaches were later repainted in the
green livery which became the standard for Green Line coaches.

Chassis details A.E.C. TYPE 662 (1–8T CLASS)

Frame   Pressed steel channel
Brakes   Vacuum servo 1/T
        1/1T, 3/1T vacuum servo/master cylinder
Rear axle   Worm axle $6\frac{1}{4}$:1, semi-floating (1T) (2/1T), $5\frac{3}{4}$:1, semi-floating (1/1T) (3/1T)
Gearbox   4 speed spur
Clutch   16″ single plate
Engine   6-cylinder 95 bhp, 100 mm. bore, 130 mm. stroke
  Note: 2/1T and 3/1T 110 mm. bore 3T—95mm. bore.
        A.E.C. Engine types 140, 145, and 137 refer.
Track   6′ 3 $\frac{3}{16}$″ front, 5′ 10 $\frac{3}{16}$″ rear
Suspension   Leaf springs
Steering   Marles
Overall length   25′ $8\frac{7}{8}$″   *Wheelbase*   17′ 0″
Overall width   Front hub 7′ $4\frac{1}{2}$″, rear wheels 7′ 4 $\frac{3}{16}$″
Turning circle   60′ 0″

Body details

Overall height   8′ $9\frac{1}{4}$″   *Overall width* 7′ 6″
Seating   30
Unladen weight 5 tons 8 cwt.*   *Laden weight* 7 tons 12 cwt. (bus)
       * Registered   8 tons 3 cwt. (Green Line)

COACHWORK
L.G.O.C., Short Bros., and Hall Lewis to T706 except 150/4 by Hoyal
Duple, Ransom & Weymann from 207–306

Vehicles built (or acquired)

T1–50 rear entrance buses, except T38 which became Exp. Green Line
T156 rear entrance bus, replacement for T38
T43 was fitted with A.E.C. 8-cylinder engine and wheelbase extended to 16′ 6″
All rebuilt except 15, 21, 25, 26 and 35 to front entrance
Oil engines later fitted to 18 vehicles and rebuilt Marshall bodies
51–149, 155, 157–206, 27 seater rear entrance Green Line (7 tons)
T150–154 private hire with sliding hood sold 1937 (8 tons). Variations of 7 tons.
T207–306 30 seater front entrance Green Line
26 of these were fitted with bodies from R class and with 7·7 litre oil engines. With the 5 othe
Weymann bodies, they became the 11T11 class
T307–318 ex Tilling. Square full-width indicator boxes. 28 seaters rebuilt to 30 later
T307–324 Coaches ex East Surrey. Hall Lewis body. 29 seater. Tilling body. F/R entrances
T325–345 ex Auto-car but transferred to Maidstone and District
T346–351 Coaches ex Blue Belle. London lorries body
T352–357 ex Queenline. London lorries body
T358–371 other independents. 358 Strachan ex Green Line, remainder Strachan & Harringtor
    bodies
T372–390 mainly rear entrance ex East Surrey owned by L.G.O.C.
During the second World War some 'T' type vehicles were converted to Producer Gas
    operation
Green Line used T307–318 for some acquired vehicles 1930/31 which duplicated the Tilling 'T'
In 1935, therefore, this group of numbers mainly in the ex East Surrey section were
renumbered T391–402.

(*Lower Right*) Front-entrance 'T' type on the Aylesbury to Edenbridge service showing the new liver
introduced in November 1935. It carried 30 passengers. The '1d fare' board carried applied to the
section of route between Oxted and Edenbridge, where the local bus was withdrawn upon the
introduction of this service in December 1934.

(*Above*) T101 in Green Line
livery at Watford Pond Cross
roads in June 1934. Note that
running letters are not carried.
J. Higham

(*Left*) T97, a coach with L.G.O.C.
27-seater body. The route board
suggests that the time is about
1936.

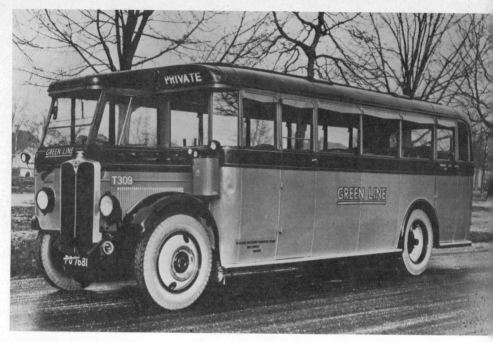

(*Above*) T309 in the pale blue/green livery of the year 1935. This ex-East Surrey vehicle was always used for Private Hire.

(*Below*) Typical 'General' 'T' type, with curved front and opening windscreen.   *Alan B. Cross*

(*Above*) 'T' type after a Marshalls rebuild following war damage. It is seen here on the stand at Feltham Station.

Alan B. Cross

(*Below*) T312, an ex-Tilling bus dating from 1929, at Malden Crossing. The revised blind display bears evidence of improvisation of the original Tilling-type indicator box by Chiswick engineers.

11 **LT Type** 1929

THE USE OF 3 AXLES for a vehicle clearly gave an increased carrying capacity as well as a better tractive characteristic. Vehicles were generally restricted by an axle weight and a third axle allowed a bigger bus to be designed. Although L.G.O.C. were not the leaders in the field, they were not far behind with their LS type introduced in 1927.

It was in 1929 that the LT type known as the A.E.C. Renown arrived. A prototype was first produced, LT1, which set the style. Seating was for 54 and an open staircase was used. When production of the first 49 was started, the seating capacity was increased to 60 but retaining the open staircase. It is believed that these vehicles used the A.E.C. 100 mm. bore engine (petrol). A further 100 followed with the same seating capacity and open stairs but with the more usual rounded driver's cab instead of the squarish version used on the first 50. Official records show that a slightly larger bore engine was used (110 mm.).

Then came the introduction of the enclosed staircase which resulted in a reduction of seating to 56, but with little other outward change. These covered the range LT151–949, but there were several variations mainly in blind display as shown in the photographs. As built, LT151–510 had just a single box covering route number and destination. LT511–850 had a lower position for the blind box, the route being shown on a board immediately above. The remainder had a more generous route display, the ultimate destination being shown in a line in the roof over the driver's cab. During overhaul the

three types became considerably intermixed. LT191–9 were built new with A.E.C. Acro oil engines, followed later by LT643, LT750–768.

From this allocation, LT741 was developed as a prototype for the next series where the upper deck was extended fully over the driver's cab giving a flush front to the vehicles. With this and the change to an angled staircase, the capacity was increased to 60 and vehicles 951–999 were built. The build continued from 1204–1416 and throughout these two disconnected batches much experimentation was done in respect of Wilson gearboxes, A.E.C. oil engines and finally Gardner 6-cylinder oil engines on LT1417–1426. Because of the larger unit these oil-engined vehicles could be easily recognized by the projecting radiator.

The bonnet numbers LT1001–1201 were used for a single-deck version of the LT (officially known as LTL). The first 50 used the A.E.C. 110 mm. engine, front entrance body and were converted to oil in 1950. Then followed 85, being a mixture of 50 similar and the remainder with the 100 mm. engine. Finally 64 more were purchased with the 100 mm. engine.

LT1427/28 were two single-deck LT supplied in 1932 to London General Country Services and passed later to the Country Department of London Transport, being transferred to the Central Area in 1944 when they were re-painted from green to red. LT1429 was an ex-Hillman private hire saloon which was given an oil engine in 1950.

The other LT to be mentioned is LT1137 which was a double-deck Green Line but with a petrol engine, later being fitted with a General Motors 2-stroke engine for a short experimental period.

During 1938/39 most of the buses between LT151–1350 had their engines changed from petrol to oil, and the displaced petrol engines were used for STL and LTC vehicles.

A much fuller account of the LT story and subsequent changes is contained in *The Development of the London Bus 1929–1933* by Gavin Martin.

(*Left*) Prototype LT1, a 54-seater with open stairs. The limited blind display was later modified to show places on the route.

(*Below*) LT (series 851 to 950) with improved blind display.

Chassis details A.E.C. 663 RENOWN (AS BUILT)

Track   Front, 6' 5⅞" rear 6' 2¾"
Overall length   26' 9⅜"
Wheelbase   16' 6"
Frame   Pressed steel channel
Front axle   I section stamping. Roller bearings
Rear axle   Worm gear 8⅓:1 (converted to 6¾:1 with 100 mm. engines)
Gearbox   4 speed spur
Clutch   Single plate 16" dia.
Engine   6-cylinder petrol 120 bhp at 2400 rpm, 110 mm. bore* × 130 mm. stroke
Steering   Marles
Brakes   Triple servo (main fleet)
Turning circle   59' 0"
* 1st 50 were 100 mm. bore

Body details

Overall height   14' 0⅞"   *Unladen weight* 6 tons 10 cwt.
Overall width 7' 6"   *Laden weight* 11 tons 19 cwt.
Seating, outside 34, inside 26
Angle of tilt 28° (top deck fully laden)
The Single-Deck Renown A.E.C. model 664 was longer (29' 1") with a correspondingly greater wheel base (18' 7"). Its seating capacity was 35.

Vehicles built

LT 1, Prototype – 54 seats – L.G.O.C. body – open stairs.
LT 2–150, 60 seats
151–950* similar to ST type body – closed stairs – 56 seats. (LT741 was prototype for next series).
LT951–999† Flush front – clash box – petrol engines – all 60 seats·
LTL 1001–1050 35 seats Single-Deck petrol 110 mm. front entrance (converted to oil 1950)
LT1052–1136 35 seats Single-Deck (50–110 mm., 35–100 mm.)
LT1137 Double-Deck Green Line coach petrol engine (110 mm. bore)
LT1138–1201 35 seats Single-Deck 100 mm. bore
LT1204–1416† continuation of 951–999 series
LT1417–1426 continuation of 951–999 series, Gardner oil engine
LT1427–1428 Ex L.G.C.S. – Single-Deck
LT1429 ex Hillman – private hire – Single-Deck. Oil engine fitted 1950

Notes:

* i *Considerable variations exist within this group, mainly in blind display, as shown in photographs*
  ii *Also 191–199 fitted with A.E.C. Acro oil engines*
  iii *439 and 448 fitted with fluid flywheels and Wilson gearboxes*
  iv *Further batch of 20 within LT501–950 also fluid transmission*
  v *Further batch of 20 within LT501–950 also oil engines, 8·8 litre*

† i *170 fitted with petrol engine, clash gearboxes and triple servo brakes (951–999)*
  ii *30 fitted with petrol engine, Daimler pre-selective gearbox and Lockheed brakes (1325–1354)*
  iii *30 fitted with 8·8 litre oil engines, clash gearboxes. Table servo brakes (1375–1404)*
  iv *20 fitted with 8·8 litre oil engines, Daimler pre-selective gearbox and Lockheed brakes (1355–1374)*

(*Top right*) This photograph, dating from 1930, shows an LT with early inadequate blind display at Windsor Castle working the Summer Sundays service 102 (Strand and Windsor).   *J. Higham*
(*Bottom right*) LT 486, with improved display blinds, in St. Albans. Although still showing the 'General' side transfers, it is in service here during early L.P.T.B. days. The route is a Summer Sundays service between Finsbury Park and St. Albans.   *W. J. Haynes*

(*Top left*) LT revised blind display. Compare with the other improvements shown on page 39.

(*Bottom left*) Prototype 'Bluebird' L.T. The name arose from the blue colour of the interior and upholstery. It never entered service as shown here, but was fitted with improved display boxes. Unpopular with the crews, owing to the difficulty of fare collection.

(*Above*) LT851, with additional route boards.

(*Below*) Single Deck LTL (coded in the LT series), a front-entrance bus of great power which proved invaluable in dealing with bus inadequacy problems. Mobile and with the same engine as the Double-Deck LT, it was known by crews as the 'scooter'.

(*Above*) One of the Bluebird petrol engined buses which always worked from Plumstead Garage.

(*Below*) LT1137 experimental Double-Deck Green Line coach which ran in Green Line service from 1931 to 1935 before transferring to Country Bus duties. A vehicle well advanced for its day (there were insufficient passengers in the early days of Green Line services to justify Double-Decks) it was withdrawn in 1942 for oil-saving reasons and remained at Hounslow Garage until destroyed in 1946.

(*Above*) A picture of nostalgia—interior of a wartime peripheral-seating LTL with leather grabs and light cones. The notices read 'The fabric on the windows is for your protection; please do not interfere with it'.

(*Below*) Rebuilt LT, by Mann Egerton, the only vehicle with an eliptical Box.   *Alan B. Cross.*

(*Above*) LT1000, a Chiswick-designed 'CC' type.

(*Bottom*) Marshalls rebuild of immediate post-war days. It is in pale red, with repositioned route stencil.

(*Right*) Single-Deck CB type. T1001 at Byfleet. Compare with illustration on page 43.   *J. Highan*

12 CC Type and CB Type 1931

THESE SIX-WHEELED VEHICLES were designed by the L.G.O.C. and under construction for some time prior to the introduction of the A.E.C. Renown (LT type). They had engines built by Meadows of 100 mm. bore × 130 mm. stroke. The first two produced were numbered LT1000 and 1051. They had 54-seat enclosed staircase bodies rather larger than the 'ST' type. LT1000 was licensed in July 1930 and LT1051 in 1931.

Two other buses were built with the same style of engine and as these appeared in 1931 they carried the later type of LT body as on LT511. These two became LT1202 and 1203.

The Meadows engines were replaced in 1932 by A.E.C. with 100 mm. bore. All four of these vehicles were disposed of in August 1939, two being used by the B.B.C. throughout the second World War.

CB Type

These experimental buses were the single-deck version of the CC class and although design had started in 1928 they did not enter service until 1931. They spent their entire life working the Kingston–Woking service 79 (later numbered 219).

Only three were built. They were numbered T1000, 1001 and 1002. All originally had Meadows petrol engines, but A.E.C. 100 mm. bore petrol engines were fitted late in 1933. All were withdrawn in 1940.

Chassis details EXPTL. BODY AND CHASSIS BY L.G.O.C. 1931 NUMBERED T1000-2

Overall length	17′ 0″
Rear axle	Fully floating. Finally 6¼:1
Gearbox	3 speed box
Engine	Meadows 100 mm. bore × 130 mm. stroke 6-cylinder, petrol

Body details

Seating	29

13 ST Type 1930

FOLLOWING THE INTRODUCTION of the A.E.C. Regent in 1929 the L.G.O.C. obtained one of the demonstration models which had a Short Bros. 48-seat open staircase body. This was given the registration number UU6610 and was passed to East Surrey who loaned it to *Autocar* for a few months. It eventually came to the Country Bus Department of London Transport and it was numbered ST1139 in 1935. The second Regent purchased by L.G.O.C. was UU6614 and numbered ST1. It had a Chiswick-built enclosed straight staircase body which seated 49. The production batch entered service in early 1930 and were numbered ST2–836. The bodies were mainly built at Chiswick (729), but there were fifty each by Strachan and Short.

There were a few exceptions. ST136, 140, 141, 157, 162 and 163 in use by National with special lowbridge bodies which were somewhat unusual in that there was a gangway on either side of the top deck to make passenger movement easier. Two similar buses operated by Amersham & District Traction Limited later became ST1089 and 1090 in the London Transport fleet.

ST379 had an all-metal body built by Metro Cammell, which later went on ST478 for a time and lastly to ST150.

The numbers ST837–1027 were given to the A.E.C. Regents taken over by London Transport in 1933 from Thomas Tilling Ltd. They had Tilling built 52-seat open staircase bodies. Then followed some acquired vehicles from four Independents: ST1028–31.

The remaining Regents in the series were Country Area buses which were not given ST numbers until 1935 and then in alphabetical order of the registrations. Many of them were L.G.O.C. owned from their introduction. The earliest of them were forty-six supplied to East Surrey in 1929. They had 48-seat bodies by Ransomes and became ST 1085–88, 1091-1132. A further batch of East Surrey buses had standard Short Bros. bodies, similar to ST1, and were numbered ST1040–1069.

ST1133-38 were 54-seat buses with Short Bros bodies taken over from Lewis Omnibus Co. Ltd. of Watford.

Finally there were twenty-three buses built for London General Country Services in 1932 and these had a large LT style body though the seating was restricted to 48. They were given numbers ST1032–39, 1070–84.

ST462, 464, and 466 were the first London buses to have the A.E.C. Acro oil engines, but these were later transferred to the LT type.

During the second World War the ST was given a second lease of life when it was found to have the most suitable engine for coal gas operation owing to the scarce supply of petrol. One hundred and seventy were converted to tow gas-producer trailers, but improvement of petrol supplies ended the full conversion programme of 540.

(*Left*) 1929; prototype ST type.

(*Below*) Production ST type. The cab is open because there were problems with the early windscreens.

Chassis details A.E.C. CHASSIS 661

Track	Front 6′ 3 $\frac{1}{16}$″, rear 5′ 10 $\frac{3}{16}$″		
Overall length	25′ 0 $\frac{3}{8}$″	*Wheelbase*	15′ 6 $\frac{1}{2}$″
Frame	Pressed steel channel		
Front axle	I section roller bearings		
Rear axle	Worm gear 6 $\frac{1}{4}$:1. Semi-floating, taper roller hubs		
Gearbox	4 speed spur gear	*Clutch*	16″ friction plate (single)
Engine	6-cylinder petrol 95 bhp		
	A.E.C. 138 and A.E.C. 140*		
	100 mm bore, 130 mm stroke		
Brakes	Vacuum-servo. Single and triple		
Suspension	Leaf springs—shock absorbers on front		
Steering	Marles (on first 300 only, worm-and-nut on next 500)		
Electrical system	12V	*Turning circle*	60′

* On the last 300 an option was listed for A.E.C. engine A145 110 mm. bore but this does not appear to hav materialized.

VARIATIONS

Chassis: The main differences affected the choice of rear axle ratio, the use of single- or triple servo assistance for the braking and the positioning of the fuel tank either nearside or offside

Body: Disregarding the odd acquisition, the body falls into one of two classes, i.e. the fully enclosed staircase L.G.O.C. type, or the Tilling open staircase.

Body details (L.G.O.C. ST)

Overall height	14′ 3″	*Overall width* 7′ 6″	
Seating outside	29	*Seating inside* 20	
Unladen weight	6 tons 11 cwt.	*Laden weight* 9 tons 14 cwt	
Angle of tilt	28° (loaded outside)		

* Later variants with angled staircase and extended upper deck over drivers canopy gave seats up to 51. Tillin ST. Out 27 In 25.

Vehicles built

ST 1 Prototype—Square cab

2–836*: 729, L.G.O.C. Body	48–51 seats
50 Strachan Body	48–51 seats
50 Short Body	48–51 seats

* excluding 136, 140, 141, 157, 162, 163, Ex National Omnibus & Transport Co; 48 seats Short Bros. bod Lowbridge; 48 seats 379. Exp all metal MCW body (1931) 49 seats.

837–1027 Tilling open stairs 52 seats

1089 and 1090 Amersham & District Traction Co. Lowbridge 48 seats

1028–31 London Independents

1032–9/1070–84 LT type body. For London General Country Services 48 seats

1040–69 Ex East Surrey. Short Bros. body

1085–1088 Ex East Surrey and 1091–1132 Ex East Surrey. Ransomes body

1133–38 Ex Lewis of Watford, Short Bros. bodywork, 54 seater

1139 Ex East Surrey open stairs, Short Bros. bodywork, 48 seater

HISTORICAL NOTE

Many ex-L.G.O.C. ST were to be converted to Producer Gas operation (almost 540). Th experiment was not successful because of service problems, and conditions improved to suc an extent that it was not necessary to carry out the whole programme.

(*Top Right*) ST264 with larger destination box, and glazed cab. The gold-based transfers applied to the first vehicles were soon replaced by the stencils.

(*Bottom right*) New all-metal ST body ST478 (once ST 379). The bus ended its life as ST150. The scene is the Royal Forest Hotel, Chingford. Note the advert. for Odol toothpaste, a popular pre-war cake paste, and the traffic advertisement carried near the offside rear wheel. The display is strange, an must be a conductor's error. Route 511A, Chingford Mount to Stratford, did not run to the Royal Fores Hotel.

W. J. Hayne

(*Top Left*) Ex-National Omnibus Company. ST 136 on loan to central buses working the 127 service, requiring lowbridge buses for the Worcester Park bridge. It has a 48-seater Short Bros. body. This bus could have been seen more often on Route 336, running from Watford High Street garage.

(*Bottom Left*) Tilling ST type, similar to that running on the Vintage Bus route in the mid-1970s.

(*Above*) ST 1083 built for London General Country Services at Croxley Green Station. *W. J. Haynes*

(*Below*) Similar STs in L.G.C.S. livery. The lighter tones were in pale blue. *J. Higham*

(*Top*) Ex-Amersham & District Lowbridge 48-seater ST; behind is a 10T10 on the 437 service.

(*Left*) ST 1139, an open stair ST bus (ex-East Surrey) carrying East Grinstead plates. This was the first of the Regent buses and spent evaluation time with East Surrey (six weeks) and with Autocar of Tunbridge Wells (3 months) before operating from Reigate until 1933. In London Transport days it could be seen running from Grays and Godstone.   *W. J. Haynes*

(*Below*) A familiar wartime scene on level-surface routes, Notice the anti-blast netting. Failures were common, sometimes the coke or the gas system, on occasions owing to the machiavellism of crews.

(*Right*) Daimler DST type in Ludgate Circus. They were confined to Harrow Weald Garage.

14 **DST** Type 1930

THREE DAIMLER CHASSIS were purchased late in 1930 to test the use of the Wilson-type gearbox in conjunction with the Daimler Sleeve valve engine. The three were numbered DST 1–3 as they were fitted with standard ST-type 49-seat bodies built at Chiswick. They spent most of their life at Harrow Weald on route 18.

Throughout 1931/32 much experimental work was done to assess these vehicles against the ST including the testing of poppet valve engine in DST3.

In 1933 London Transport acquired two other double-deck Daimlers, first a CF6 from Eagle Bus Company and this was numbered DST4. The other, a CH6, came from the Redline Company and this was numbered DST5.

DST6 was a 32-seater coach which was taken over from another company and was allocated to the Private Hire Department. It was disposed of in 1938.

DST4 was sold in 1934 and the chassis of DST1–3/5 were sold in 1935, but the bodies were refitted to some specially shortened STL chassis which were numbered STL1260–3 though not in that order.

Chassis details MAKER'S REF: CH6 6

Track	6' 2"
Frame	Channel suction
Front axle	I Section. Taper roller bearings, thrust button support
Rear axle	6¼:1 (DST experimentally 7¼:1 for period)
Gearbox	Pre-selective Armstrong Siddeley
Clutch	Fluid flywheel
Engine	Daimler petrol CH6. Coil ignition. 97 mm. bore × 130 mm. stroke
Suspension	Leaf spring with shock absorbers all round
Steering	Marles cam and roller
Brakes	Drum brakes—separate shoes for handbrake, servo assistance

Body details

Unladen weight 6 tons 2 cwt.   *Laden weight* 9 tons 9 cwt.
Seating: 49   DST 4: 56   DST 5: 52   DST 6: 32
Angle of tilt 28·5°

Vehicles built

DST 1–3 Bought for trial of fluid transmission
DST 4 Ex Eagle Bus Co. Hildreth Garage W10 10.11.33
DST 5 Ex Redline (Brickwood Ltd.) 1933
DST 6 32 seat coach (1931) Single-Deck from West London Coaches
All chassis, except DST 6 (1938) were disposed of in 1935 and bodies (except 1, 3/5) fitted to special STL chassis.

15 H Type 1929

THE L.G.O.C. PURCHASED three Dennis 'H' type for experimental purposes in 1929. They had 50-seat open top bodies and were numbered at the end of an earlier Dennis series as D146, 147 and 148. At first allocated to Putney Bridge for routes 14 and 96, they were transferred to Overground Ltd. in 1931. When taken over by London Transport they were renumbered DH1–3.

DH4–11 were other Dennis H type acquired in 1933 from independent operators. All had been withdrawn by 1935.

Chassis details VEHICLE TYPE DENNIS H

Track	6' 5"
Overall length	
Wheelbase	16' 6"
Clutch	Cone
Engine	Dennis 4-cylinder, 30 hp, 110 mm. bore × 150 mm. stroke

Body details

Seating	50

Vehicles built DH 1–3. Previously D146, 147 and 8

(*Left*) Special shortened-wheelbased Bus (STL1260), fitted with a body from DST3. It was built in 1936, and seen here in need of major overhaul at Chiswick after some years' service.

(*Above*) Dennis H type, at Hadley Highstone (Two Brewers), in 1934, after renumbering by London Transport. An open-top, normal-control bus, it was built by the L.G.O.C. in 1929, and first ran on Route 96 (Putney to Redbridge). *J. Higham*

16 DL Type 1931

TWENTY-FIVE Dennis Lance buses were obtained by the L.G.O.C. for use by Overground Ltd., an L.G.O.C. subsidiary, and were delivered in 1931/32. They had 49-seat all-metal bodies by Metro-Cammell similar to that fitted to the experimental ST379 about six months earlier. The chassis was the standard Lance made by Dennis Bros. Ltd. of Guildford. They were numbered D 1–25 in the Overground fleet, but on being taken over by London Transport in 1933 were re-numbered DL1–25. They spent most of their life at Potters Bar, but in 1936 were sent for a short time to Sutton Garage and were sold prematurely in 1937.

DL26–33 were Dennis Lances taken over by London Transport in 1933/1934 from five independent operators.

Chassis details VEHICLE: DENNIS LANCE

Track	Front 6′ 4″. rear 5′ 10½″
Overall length	25′ 7″
Wheelbase	16′ 6″
Frame	Pressed steel channel with tubular cross members
Front axle	Reversed Elliott. Taper roller bearings
Rear axle	Underslung worm 6¾:1. Fully floating
Gearbox	Four forward
Clutch	Dry multi plate
Engine	6-cylinder petrol, overhead cam, 100 mm. bore × 130 mm. stroke, 6,126 c.c. 49 bhp at 100 rpm, 100 bhp at 2500 rpm
Suspension	Semi-elliptic leaf
Brakes	Vacuum servo-assisted, drum
Turning	58′
Steering	Marles cam-and-lever

Body details

Overall height		*Unladen weight*	9 tons 10 cwt.
Overall width	7′ 5½″	*Laden weight*	12 tons 11 cwt. 8 lb.
Seating, inside	20		
Seating, outside	29		

Vehicles built

1–25 new body (similar to metal ST vehicle)
26–33 Additions from independent operators with different body builders

(Top right) Dennis Lance, built in 1931 for Overground Ltd., it appears here in early L.P.T.B. livery, with 'General' fleet name, in use before adoption of London Transport transfer.

(Bottom Right) Dennis Dart bus. An 18 seater. Note the practice of using only one headlight. See page 58 for description.

17 DA Type and other one-man buses 1931

TO OPEN UP new routes where the traffic was expected to be sparse at least at the start, some Dennis Dart vehicles were purchased which were to be one-man-operated. Providing the seating capacity was not more than 20, it was possible to use this form of operation at that time.

The first series comprised 20 and 12 respectively on the same type of chassis, the difference in the body being of greater height (about 8″) for the first 20. In each case perimeter seating was employed giving a capacity of 18.

On the next 8 more conventional seating was employed and only 2 longitudinal seat of 3 on the front at either side.

Finally the last 2 vehicles reverted to perimeter seating again with a total capacity of 17 mainly because of a vehicle width reduction to 6′ 6″.

All these vehicles were allocated to Central area duties.

BEAN
A single-deck normal control Bean with 18-seat body was bought in 1930 for a local service to Pinner Golf Club operated by Winter's Taxi Service which ran as 'Pinner Bus'

(*Below*) A rare photograph of the little-known Bean bus acquired from the Royal Highlander Company (Mrs. Sayers) and run from Harrow Weald Garage on the short route from Pinner to Pinner Hill Golf Club. It is at Pinner Green. *W. Noel Jackson*

t was taken over by L.G.O.C. six months later but withdrawn in 1931. The bus later became a van for Morden Station Garage.

LANCIA

Four small Lancia buses were obtained in 1925 and operated by National, and numbered L1–4. All were withdrawn in 1930.

GUY

Six Guy BA20s were bought for National operation in 1928 and they were numbered G3–8. They were normal control 20-seaters and operated mainly in the Watford area. They were withdrawn in 1934. G1–2 were former Independent buses transferred to National.

MORRIS

Eight Morris Viceroys were obtained in 1931 and six were sent to East Surrey as buses. The other two operated as Green Line coaches. All had 20-seat front entrance bodies. In 1935 the buses were numbered MS4–9 and the coaches MS10 and 11. All were withdrawn by 1937.

COMMER

Six Commer Invaders were ordered by L.G.O.C. in 1931 for Green Line but only two were actually used for that purpose, the others passing to East Surrey as buses. The two coaches quickly followed suit. They had 18-seat front entrance bodies and were used in various parts of the Country Area. They were replaced by the Leyland Cubs in 1935.

Chassis details MAKER'S REF: DENNIS DART 1931

Track	Front 4' 10⅜", rear 5' ⅛"
Overall length	(i) 20' 10¹⁵⁄₁₆". (ii) 20' 6¹¹⁄₁₆". (iii) 20' 3¹¹⁄₁₆"
Wheelbase	13' 2¾" all vehicles
Frame	Pressed steel channel
Front axle	'H' section. Taper roller bearings, width over hub caps 6' 1¼"
Rear axle	Worm gear 6·2:1, width over hub caps 6' 1¼"
Gearbox	4-speed spur gears
Clutch	Single plate
Engine	6-cylinder petrol, 85 mm. bore, 120 mm. stroke. Electric starter
Suspension	Leaf spring
Brakes	Single servo
Turning circle	60'

Body details

ST SERIES

Overall height	(i) 8' 11⅜" (ii) 8' 3¼"	*Overall width*	7' 2"
Unladen weight	3 tons 15 cwt.	*Laden weight*	5 tons

2ND SERIES

Overall height	8' 5⅞"	*Overall width*	7' 2"
Seating, 1st & 2nd series	18		

3RD SERIES

Overall height	8' 7⅝"	*Overall width*	6' 6"
Seating	17		

Vehicles built

1st series 32 (2 body variations) both perimeter seating
2nd series 8 conventional seating
3rd series 2 (narrower body, 6' 6"). Perimeter seating

(*Above*) A former East Surrey Morris Viceroy bus in 1934.

(*Below*) A former National Guy BA20 single-decker at Watford. Note there is no route number shown. Many buses taken over from independent operators in the 1930s ran for some time without numbers. Behind is an ex 'National' ADC bus. *J. Higham*

Chassis details VEHICLE TYPE GUY–G. MAKER'S REF: BA (*See lower illustration opposite*)

Track	5' 11¼"
Overall length	
Wheelbase	14' 1" (could be 13' 4")
Frame	Dropped frame
Engine	4·5 litre, 4-cylinder, 4" bore × 5½" stroke

Body Details

Seating	20

Vehicles built

G 3–8 for National
G1 and 2 were former independents transferred to this class

Summary of other one-man buses

Lancia PENTAIOTA 30 hp engine, 110 mm. bore × 130 mm. stroke. Dry plate clutch. 4-speed gearbox. Wheelbase 15' 6"
Morris VICEROY 6-cylinder engine, 85 mm. bore × 125 mm. stroke
Commer INVADER GTK 6-cylinder engine, 24 hp, 80 mm. bore × 116 mm. stroke, 13' 6" wheelbase, track 5' 2⅞"

(*Below*) Commer Invader in Sevenoaks High Street, about 1932. The vehicle was one of six operated by East Surrey. *J. Higham*

(*Above*) Morris Viceroy coach, repainted in early Green Line livery.

(*Below*) STL1, the prototype STL bus. Its box-like body holds 60 seats. It entered service on Route 8 (not 63 as the blinds indicate).

18 STL Type (LGOC & early LPTB) 1932

THE NEED FOR a six-wheeled vehicle to hold 56 to 60 passengers ceased early in 1932 when the Ministry of Transport extended the permitted wheelbase length for a four-wheeled double-deck bus from 15 ft. 6½ in. to 16 ft. 3 in. The STL vehicle was the logical development and the opportunity was taken to use the longer wheelbase and also to extend the upper deck completely over the driver's cab making a 60-seat capacity vehicle.

The first fifty vehicles introduced by the L.G.O.C. in 1933 were in two distinct batches of 24 and 26, the first having the semi-floating axle and the latter, what was to become the all time standard, fully-floating, so relieving the driving shafts of bending loads. These were numbered STL1–50.

Another fifty buses to a similar style were also delivered in 1933 and these were numbered STL153–202 due to the intervening numbers being allotted to an order for Tilling buses as detailed in the next section. Because of minor differences the latter vehicles were coded 2STL.

In 1933 the capacity of the vehicle was reduced at the design stage to 56 and the London Passenger Transport Board started to build its first bus. The vehicle employed a greater slope at each end, so getting away from the box effect of earlier L.G.O.C. STL but which reduced the upper deck capacity by four. There were 50 of these, STL203–252.

(*Below*) Petrol-engined STL, with Fluid transmission. Tottenham and Chalk Farm shared the allocation of the new buses of this type.

having the pre-selective gearbox which had been tried out on STL50 earlier. There were modifications to the engine which produced a variant in the chassis code from 3STL to 1/3STL.

Then followed a mixed batch of 350 vehicles. The first 39 utilised the 110 mm. petrol engines displaced from the LT that were in the process of being converted to oil. These were grouped as 4STL(36) and 1/4STL(3). Next were 50 in the 6STL class which introduced the Lockheed servo braking system, but a petrol engine from the LT conversion (292–341). The next 11 vehicles STL342–352 do not belong in this category as they were the first indirect injection oil engines in this class. A repeat order of 50 took the series from STL 353 to 402.

By this time A.E.C. were making a pre-selector gearbox which replaced the Daimler version and 200 buses in the 7STL class were added (STL403–552) and 559–608.

The missing numbers, STL553–557, were allocated to A.E.C. Regent chassis fitted with open top bodies (53 seats) previously operated by Charles Pickup of Dulwich. Two years later they were fitted with the standard enclosed top decks. The other missing number, 558, was allocated to a Regent chassis with 50-seat Birch body from Redline. This was fitted with a Daimler pre-selective gearbox. All six were taken over by London Transport in 1933, together with other vehicles.

Chassis details MAKER'S REF: A.E.C. 661/-SERIES

Track	Front 6′ 3 $\frac{1}{16}$″, rear 5′ 10 $\frac{3}{16}$″
Overall length	25′ 5 $\frac{3}{8}$″
Wheelbase	16′ 3″
Frame	Pressed steel channel
Front axle	I section roller bearing
Rear axle	Worm gear 6 $\frac{1}{4}$:1 fully floating (apart from 24).
Gearbox	4-speed spur gear
Clutch	Friction plate
Engine	6-cylinder petrol, 100 mm. bore, 130 mm. stroke, 95 hp A.E.C. 162
Brakes	Lockheed servo-assisted

Suspension	Leaf spring	Steering	Marles
Electrical system	24 volt	Turning circle	60′

Body details

Overall height	13′ 11 $\frac{3}{4}$″	Overall width	7″ 6″
Unladen weight	5 tons 18 cwt.	Laden weight	9 tons 16 cwt.
Seating, outside	34	Seating, inside	26
Angle of tilt	28°		

Vehicles built

(1STL1) STL1–50 L.G.O.C. 60 seaters. Chiswick body. (STL50 was fitted with a pre-selective gearbox)

(2STL1) STL153–202 with pre-selective gearbox

(3STL2) STL203–252 L.P.T.B. 56 seaters with Daimler pre-selective gearbox. Later converted to 16STL.

(4STL3) STL253–291 L.P.T.B. 56 seaters with Daimler pre-selective gearbox. Later converted to 1/16STL. (3 later converted to clash 1/4STL.)

(6STL3) STL292–341, 353–402. Conventional 661 chassis

(7STL3) STL403–552, 559–608. Also fitted with A.E.C. pre-selector transmission D132. (Converted to 2/16STL.)

(12STL8) STL553–557. 53 seater ex pickup with open top. P.R.V. body. Chiswick top fitted. Clash gearbox.

(13STL9) STL 558. Ex Red Line 50 seater. Birch body. Fitted with pre-selective gearbox.

19 STL Type (Tilling) 1932

THE L.G.O.C. had ordered 102 STLs to replace the ageing petrol-electric buses operated on their behalf by Thomas Tilling. These buses, allocated numbers STL51–152, were built by Tillings with a 56-seat body to its own design. Delivery started late in 1932 and continued during the first six months of 1933 but ceased on the formation of London Transport in July that year. The order for the last twenty-two was cancelled and numbers STL131–152 were never used.

Although the body design was a little more advanced than the L.G.O.C. counterpart, the chassis was more in line with the L.G.O.C. STL. Semi-floating axles were used and the smaller A.E.C. engine with 12 volt electrical supply system.

They always worked from the former Tilling garages at Catford (TL), Croydon (TC) and Bromley (TB). Twenty of these buses were lost in the 1941 Croydon fire, the rest being withdrawn by 1951.

Chassis details MAKER'S REF: A.E.C. 661/-SERIES TILLING—PETROL (8STL)

Track	Front 6' 3 1/16", rear 5' 10 3/16"		
Overall length	25' 8⅝"	*Wheelbase*	16'
Frame	Pressed steel channel		
Front axle	I section		
Rear axle	Worm gear 6¼:1 semi-floating		
Gearbox	4-speed spur		
Clutch	Friction plate		
Engine	6-cylinder petrol, 95 mm. bore, 130 mm. stroke, A.E.C. 137		
Brakes	Lockheed servo assisted		
Suspension	Leaf springs	*Steering*	Marles
Electrical system	12 volt	*Turning circle*	60'

Body details

Overall height	13' 11½"	*Seating, outside*	30
Overall width	7' 6"	*Seating, inside*	26
Laden weight	9 tons 19 cwt.		

Vehicles built

8ST4 Code, STL51–130, 56 seater, Tilling body. Remainder of batch (22) cancelled.

20 STL Type (Oil engine)

ELEVEN VEHICLES of the earlier series were fitted with the A.E.C. 7·7 litre indirect-injection oil engine and Wilson pre-selector gearbox and were coded 5STL (STL342–352). From an external point of view there was little difference between the two types. The follow up of this experimental batch came with STL609–758. By this time the body had taken the L.P.T.B. shape which was to remain fairly standard for the bulk of the

(*Above*) Typical Thomas Tilling STL bus. Petrol-engined, with tiny side number display, they were first used on Route 36 (West Kilburn to Hither Green).

(*Below*) First conventional oil-engined STL. First built in 1934, most deliveries of this batch went to Merton and replaced the LTs and aging NS types on all routes running from this garage.

remainder of this fleet. These were known as the 9STL, and a repeat order followed (759–958) with only a change to tubular seating. These were referred to as 1/9STL.

Then came the change to a forward entrance design for the country area. These were fitted with an LT-designed body, but only carried 52 passengers because of the forward staircase. These carried the numbers STL959–1043 and 1056–1059 (10 STL coding).

The missing numbers were allocated to what were referred to as the Godstone STL. Originally ordered by L.G.C.S. they could be called the 'Reigate' version of the Chiswick forward entrance previously mentioned. However, they differed in that a sliding door was fitted to the entrance and the 8·8 litre oil engine was used with a clash gearbox. They were built by Weymann to the lowbridge pattern, to pass under a railway bridge on Route 410. Probably for convenience these were coded in the STL series as 11STL.

The next STL series 1060–1259 had minor changes to the destination lay out at the front but otherwise maintained the same oil engine and pre-selector gearbox. Since these were similar in many ways to the 1/9STL, another sub-division was used namely 2/9STL.

STL1260–1263 were short wheelbase STL chassis utilised for 4 DST bodies when Daimler CH6 chassis were sold in 1935. For identification purposes these were known as 14STL.

STL 1264–1463 and 1514–1613 covered the next two orders. Although the chassis coding was 3/9STL the variation of an improved fluid flywheel was fitted to the last 100.

The intervening numbers were used for a further delivery of the forward entrance STL but with metal bodies built by Weymann. Those vehicles were classified 1/10 STL.

With STL1614 a change occurred in that the route number was moved to the roof and this continued until STL2515 but with the usual variations. A group of 40 vehicles were fitted with special bodies for the Blackwall and Rotherhithe Tunnel services but not consecutive. The other variation was covered by 175 coded 4/9 STL as this batch was fitted with Park Royal all-metal construction bodies.

With the next 132 vehicles a change was made to the engine in that direct injection was employed with a fully flexible engine mounting; they were coded as 15 and 1/15STL. This took the STL class to 2647, delivery completing in 1939.

For record purposes the conversion of various quantities of 3, 4, and 7 STL chassis must be mentioned. These were originally fitted with petrol engines, but were later fitted with A.E.C. direct injection oil engines in 1938 and took 16, 1/16, and 2/16 chassis codings.

In 1941–42 L.P.T.B. purchased some standard A.E.C. chassis and mounted them with bodies from other vehicles once they had injected into the float some 34 new bodies. These were clash gearbox type of vehicles and in consequence required another coding, that of 17STL. Twenty new lowbridge bodies of utility construction were fitted to the earlier 9STL chassis.

Because of a severe shortage of buses after the war 20 standard A.E.C. chassis were purchased similar to 17STL but were fitted with the post-war Weymann body (see Chapter 34).

In 1942 a start was made on converting the indirect-injection oil engines in the earlier STL to the now generally accepted direct-injection engine.

In 1935 STF1 appeared, a fully fronted bus renumbered STL857 for a time, but it only lasted in this form until 1938.

Experiments were conducted in 1945 with STL2284 modified as a Pay-as-You-enter bus with separate exit and entrance—the first time such an experiment had been made. After operational trials on Route 65 it was found to be too slow in operation.

One further STL should be mentioned STL2477 known as the 'Sainsbury STL' which was fitted with a new type easily detachable body panelling at the end of the war and ran for a short time for evaluation. This marked the end of an era and development work on the STL. It was the close of a great chapter in London bus development.

Chassis details MAKER'S REF: A.E.C. 0661/-SERIES. L.P.T.B.—OIL ENGINE (5STL)

Track	6′ 5⅜″, rear 5′ 10 3/16″		
Overall length	25′ 5⅜″	*Wheelbase*	16′ 3″
Frame	Pressed channel nickel steel		
Front axle	I Section	*Rear axle*	Worm 5¾:1 fully floating
Gearbox	Wilson pre-selective		
Clutch	Fluid flywheel		
Engine	6-cylinder, 105 mm. bore, 146 mm. stroke, A.E.C. 171 (ind. inj.), 108 bhp (converted to A173 direct injection)		
Brakes	Lockheed servo assisted	*Suspension*	Leaf springs
Steering	A.E.C. worm and nut	*Electrical system*	24 volt
Turning circle	60′		

Body details

Overall height	13′ 11½″	*Unladen weight*	6 tons 18 cwt.
Overall width	7′ 6″	*Laden weight*	9 tons 19 cwt.
Seating, outside	30	Body L.P.T.B. with tubular seat frames	
Seating, inside	26		

Vehicles built

342–352	5STL	3/1	11	
609–758	9STL	5	150	
759–958	1/9STL	5/1		
		& 2	200	
1060–1259	2/9STL	11	200	
1264–1463	3/9STL	11	200	
1514–1613	3/9STL	11	100	
1614–	4/9STL	14	150	Roof route number box
	4/9STL	14	204	Roof route number box
	4/9STL	13	40	Tunnel bus 55 seater
	4/9STL	12	6	As STL5/2
2014–2188	4/9STL	15	175	PRV body
	4/9STL	14/1	233	As STL 11
–2515	4/9STL	12	94	As STL 5/2
959–1043	10STL	6	89	Country area F/E Wooden body 52 seater
1056–1059				
1464–1513	1/10STL	6/1	50	Country area F/E Weymann metal body 52 seater
1044–1055	11STL	7	12	(8·8 litre (Clash GB) Country area F/E Weymann lowbridge body. 48 seater, L.G.O.C. order)
1260–1263	14STL	10	4	Ex DST. body. 48 seater
2516–2647	15STL	16	⎫ 132	
	1/15STL	16/1	⎭	
	16STL	18/1	50	Ex. 3STL petrol conversion STL 2 body. Fitted with A173 DI after original petrol (1938)
	1/16STL/	8/	36	Ex 4STL petrol conversion STL 3/2 body. Fitted with A173 DI after original petrol (1938)
	2/16STL	18	200	Ex 5STL petrol conversion STL 3/2 body. Fitted with A173 DI after original petrol (1938)
2648–2681	17STL		34	All types of body on W/T chassis. (14 wartime body either STL17 or 17/1).
	STL	19	20	Low bridge bodies on existing chassis. Odd numbers. 53 seater
2682–2701	18STL	20	20	Weymann post-war. (See 18STL 20 and 14T12 section 34.) Clash gearbox.

(*Above*) STL857 which became STF1.
A landmark in experimental STL design before the war, it ran for some years before being restored to the familiar STL style.

(*Left*) Country area STL, with front entrance and unusual centrally-placed staircase. They were cold for passengers and troubled by windswept litter scooped into the body.

(*Top Left*) STL with 8·8 oil engine, nicknamed 'Godstone' STL buses because these vehicles were lowbridge and allocated to Godstone garage for the route passing under Oxted bridge.

(*Bottom Left*) The flowering of the STL design. This bus type appeared during 1935–36.

(*Above*) STL type built for use in Rotherhithe and Blackwall tunnels. The staircase turned a full 180° in the rise, the bodies were convex in shape, and the buses were fitted with special anti-scuff tyres.

(*Below*) STL 1954, a lowbridge bus appearing in 1942. Twelve were allocated to Harrow Weald Garage for use on the Route 230. The low bridge is at Headstone Drive.

(*Above*) STL with P.R.V. metal body. The bodies suffered from corrosion problems and were scrapped in 1948.

(*Bottom*) The London bus in wartime—a wartime chassis with pre-war body, showing how the full windows were replaced with boards during the worst of the London bombing attacks.

Above) 1946, and experiments start with Pay-as-you-enter buses. This STL was converted in Chiswick, with separate doors, an unusual central staircase, and the small pay booth (like a cinema pay-desk) where a seated conductor issued tickets. Large queues not used to this novel approach to revenue collection made the idea a failure; Ealing Broadway was a bad place for this sort of thing.

Below) Front-entrance country bus converted to Tree Lopping duties. The drop side on the upper deck was for debris-clearance.

(*Above*) The last STL development—the 'Sainsbury' STL. It worked only from Alperton Garage

(*Right*) The prototype Leyland Cub. (C.I.) at Sunbury War Memorial. Note the front fender carried by early buses.

21 C Type 1934

TO PROVIDE a one-man bus to replace the Dennis Dart and other non-standard small buses acquired from Independent operators, a prototype vehicle numbered C1 was produced on a Leyland Cub chassis with petrol engine. It was used in the Central Area from introduction in October 1934 until 1935 when it was transferred to Country Area. A Perkins indirect-injection oil engine was fitted in 1935.

The year 1935 saw the introduction of seventy-four of these vehicles (C2–75) fitted with a twenty-seat Short Bros. body instead of the Chiswick body as on C1. They employed the Leyland 4·4 litre direct-injection six-cylinder engine. They were required to open up new routes in the Country Area and to replace a variety of acquired secondhand small vehicles.

C76 was a Leyland KP3 acquired from St. Albans & District in 1933 and withdrawn in 1938.

In order to replace the Dennis Dart and other small vehicles in the Central Area another twenty-two Cubs were obtained in 1936 (C77–98). They employed the Leyland 4·7 indirect-injection engines and had a Weymann body of similar appearance to the earlier Cubs.

In the same year eight one and half-decker petrol-engined Cubs were purchased for the London Interstation service. The earlier Cubs had all been normal control but these were forward control. They had 20-seat Park Royal front-entrance observation coach bodies with extensive luggage space below the raised rear portion—an unusual bus design. They were based at Old Kent Road (P). After a break during the war years they returned to Interstation duties from 1946–1950.

The missing numbers were, in fact, lorries at first numbered C99–105, but later allocated numbers 180C–186C with the service fleet.

The Leyland Cub was a most useful and popular small bus type and many continued in service until 1953.

Below) Cub C83. A Central area bus running from Barking Garage and transferred later to Hornchurch. *J. Higham*

75

Chassis details MAKER'S REF: LEYLAND CUB KPO3

Track	5' 7" front, 5' 5⅛" rear	*Clutch*	Dry plate single
Overall length	23' 11⅞" (interstation 23')	*Engine*	6-cylinder, 3½" bore, 5½" stroke
Wheelbase	15' 6"	*(C2–75)*	60 bhp oil engine
Frame	Channel	*Brakes*	Lockheed m/cyl.
Front axle	I section. Roller bearings	*Suspension*	Leaf spring
Rear axle	Worm 6½:1	*Steering*	Cam-and-roller
Gearbox	4-speed clash		

Body details

NORMAL CONTROL (C1–98)

Overall height	8' 3⅞" laden	*Overall width* 7' 5"	
Unladen weight	3 tons 19 cwt.	*Laden weight* 5 tons 7 cwt.	
Seating	20		

FORWARD CONTROL (C106–113) INTERSTATION

Overall height	10' 4 3/16"	*Overall width* 7" 6"	
Unladen weight	4 tons 17 cwt	*Laden weight* 6 tons 6 cwt.	
Seating	18		

Vehicles built

1934 C1. Petrol engine (Leyland) changed later to Perkins I.D.I.
1935 C2–75. D.I. oil engine 4·4 litre 60 bhp (KP03). Short Bros. body.
1936 C76. Transfer from St. Albans & District
1936 C77–98. 4.7 litre I.D.L. oil engine. Body by Weymanns (65 bhp).
1936 C106–113. 1½ Decker. Petrol 4·7 litre Leyland. 85·7 mm. bore × 127 mm. stroke.
(SKPZ2) Petrol engine, 18 seater. P.R.V. body
Missing numbers were lorries later allocated fleet numbers 180–186C and 202C

(*Below*) Leyland Cub with Short Bros. body. This bus ran from Hertford garage on Route 342 for many years, working the short journeys on Route 303 between Potters Bar and New Barnet between scheduled 342 journeys. Here it carries the Bishops Stortford Garage code, cut but never used on service buses; by the time the plates were available the garage had closed.

(*Right*) Petrol-engined Cub (C106). Operating from Old Kent Road Garage, these buses worked the Inter-station service, scheduled for fast running.

22 Q Type 1932

THE YEAR 1932 saw the birth of a revolutionary new design: the Q type. It had a normal oil engine mounted slightly inclined on the offside of the chassis. This enabled the whole of the body area to be utilised for seating purposes giving an improvement over the normal thirty for a conventional single-decker. Q1 was, in fact, a thirty-seven seat single-decker with petrol engine and clash gearbox. It entered service in September 1932 on the busy Central Area route 11, but a month later it went on to the Peckham circular route (621, now P3), and passed to the Country Area in 1934.

Q2 and 3 were double-deckers with front entrances for the Central Area new in 1934. They had Chiswick-built 56-seat bodies and even by today's standard were many years before their time, with gracious curves that presented a far better street image than current designs. From an engineering standpoint advances in tyre design enabled the use of only four wheels instead of six. Both passed to the Country Area in 1937.

Q4 and 5 were similar double-deckers for the Country Area, but they had Weymann 56-seat centre-entrance bodies with air-operated sliding doors. Q3 was lost by war action in 1941, the others being sold in 1946.

Production vehicles began to flow in 1935 with single-deck country buses with centre exit. They had 37-seat bodies by Birmingham Railway Carriage and Wagon Co., and were numbered Q6–105/186–7.

A Central Area version with front entrance and without a door arrived in 1936. These were Q106–185. They had 37-seat all-metal bodies by Park Royal. Although all eighty were intended for the Central Area, twenty-seven were loaned to the Country Area, but subsequently transferred to the Central Area. All these single-deck buses were withdrawn by 1953.

Finally, a Green Line version appeared late in 1936, Q189–238. The body was again by Park Royal and the now familiar slope of the roof line had disappeared giving a more

customary appearance. They seated 32 and had front entrance with sliding doors. After use as ambulances during the war years they returned to Green Line work until replaced by the RF coaches in 1951/52. Twenty-four were transferred early in 1952 to Muswell Hill to take over from the time expired LTL until the RF appeared later in the year.

The final development of the Q class was a six-wheeler three-axled double-deck Green Line coach with petrol engine, hydraulic transmission and electrically-operated gearbox. This was Q188 which entered experimental service in 1937, but it was found unsuitable for Green Line service and so it became a Country Area bus until 1940.

Other than by one or two far-seeing operators, the Q did not find favour and production ceased in 1936.

Chassis details MAKER'S REF: A.E.C. CHASSIS O762

Track	Front 6′ 6″, rear 6′ 6″
Overall length	27′ 5″
Wheelbase	18′ 6″
Frame	Channel
Front axle	Beam
Rear axle	5·4:1 worm offset
Gearbox	4-speed pre-selective
Clutch	Fluid flywheel
Engine	6-cylinder oil engine A170 Ricardo. Combustion head. 106 mm. bore, 146 mm. stroke. 123 bhp at 2300 rpm
Brakes	Lockheed servo
Suspension	Semi-elliptic leaf spring
Steering	Worm-and-nut

Body details

BUS

(i) *Overall height* 9′ 1″   *Overall width* 7′ 5″, *seats* 34
   Unladen weight 5 tons 12 cwt.

(ii) *Overall height* 9′ 8⅝″   *Overall width* 7′ 6″, *seats* 37

COACH

   Overall height 9′ 11⅝″   *Overall width* 7′ 6″, *seats* 32

Vehicles built

1935–6	4Q4 Q 6–80 75 Country bus. Middle door. B.R.C.W. body
	1/4Q4/1 81–105, 186 & 7 Country bus. Middle door. B.R.C.W. body
1936	5Q5 Q 106–185 53 Central bus. Front entrance. P.R.V.
	1/5Q5/1 27 27 Central bus. Front entrance. P.R.V.
1936	6Q6 Q 189–238 50 Coach. P.R.V.

Special types

1932 Q1 Single-Deck bus, petrol engine crash gearbox
    Q2 Front entrance Double-Deck. Self-change Daimler gearbox
    Q3 Front entrance Double-Deck. Self-change Daimler gearbox
    Q4 Centre entrance Double-Deck Weymann body. A.E.C. pre-selective box
    Q5 Centre entrance Double-Deck Weymann body. A.E.C. pre-selective box
    Q188 Double-Deck Green Line coach.

(*Below right*) Front entrance double-deck bus (Q2) with Daimler pre-selective gearbox. It never ran on Route 77 but was attached with Q3 to Harrow Weald for route 114. Later it ran on route 52 (from Middle Row) and subsequently passed to the Country area.

78

(*Above*) Q1, with petrol engine and clash
gearbox. Note large fares board obscured by
grab-rail.

(*Above*) Central-entrance (and central staircase) body by Weymann. The bus is Q4. Built in 1934, it spent most of its life at Leatherhead garage on Route 406.

(*Left*) Country area Q type, with Birmingham Railway Carriage Co. body

(*Below*) Central area Q129, with Park Royal body. These buses, loading forward of the front wheel, proved dangerous with the London crowds if they attempted to alight when the bus was turning, as the front wheel moved clear of the bus.

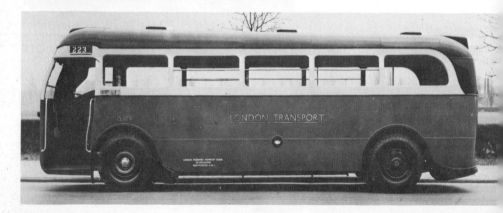

(*Above*) Experimental coach Q188 later demoted to Country bus.

(*Below*) Green Line Q coach, with dummy radiator put on the body to avoid misunderstandings from passengers waiting for the coach—it was hard to tell in which direction an almost static coach would run! This has a Weymann body and carries Leavesden Road plates.

23 **9T9 Type** 1936

THE **9T9** may be considered in the first instance as a single-deck version of the 1936 STL vehicle. As it was intended for Country bus operation (including coaches), the body and seating were more luxurious. In fact, the front end of the vehicle had the tendency towards a partial streamlined look. In consequence the overall weight of the vehicle was a little higher in proportion to its double-deck counterpart and at times the A.E.C. 7·7 litre engine was over-taxed.

Fifty such vehicles were built in 1936 and the overall appearance marked a step forward in design. All were withdrawn by 1951.

Chassis details MAKER'S REF: A.E.C. 0662 SERIES

Overall length	27′ 6″
Wheelbase	17′ 6″
Frame	Channel
Front axle	I section taper roller bearings
Rear axle	Worm 5·1/5:1. Fully floating
Gearbox	A.E.C. pre-selective 4-speed
Clutch	Fluid flywheel
Engine	A.E.C. 7·7 oil engine A173, 105 mm. bore × 146 mm. stroke
Brakes	Lockheed servo
Suspension	Leaf springs

Body details

Overall height	9′ 11¾″	*Unladen weight*	6 tons 13 cwt.
Overall width	7′ 6″	*Laden weight*	8 tons 17 cwt.
Seats	30		

Vehicles built   T403–452 30-seat Country bus/coach. Weymann body

(*Below*) 9T9 coach, backbone (with the 10T10) of Green Line services in the last years of the 30s. This one carries Leavesden Road plates (an old 'General' garage) and has a Weymann body.

24 STD Type 1937

IN 1937 AN order was placed with Leyland for 100 double-deck vehicles with metal bodies following the STL external features. The bonnet letters STD are thought to have come from a combination of the S from STL and TD from the Leyland type Titan TD4. The first ninety vehicles were fitted with the standard Leyland arrangement of 8·6 litre oil engine with a clash 4 speed constant mesh gearbox and dry plate clutch; the remaining 10 employing a Lysholm-Smith torque convertor. This enabled a comparison to be made between the two transmissions which showed the clash box to be superior and at a later date the 10 were converted to standard.

These handsome vehicles spent the majority of their working life on routes allocated to Hendon garage (AE) and could always be recognised by the deep throb of their engines. It was not until the last years that the pride of the drivers in giving a smooth and quiet ride began to evaporate and the requests were made for a pre-selective transmission bus to cope with the post-war boom in traffic.

(*Below*) Leyland STD bus, with Leyland all-metal body. These buses were always associated with Hendon garage and produced reliability from their deep-throated engines.

Chassis details MAKER S REF: LEYLAND TD4

Overall length	25′ 11″
Wheelbase	16′ 6″
Frame	Channel
Front axle	I section taper roller
Rear axle	Worm 5.4:1 taper roller, fully floating
Gearbox	Clash 4-speed. Constant mesh 3rd
Clutch	Dry plate (single)
Engine	8·6 litre oil engine, $4\frac{1}{2}″$ bore, $5\frac{1}{2}″$ stroke, 58 bhp at 1000 rpm
Brakes	Lockheed servo. 2″ master cylinder
Suspension	Leaf spring. Shock absorbers front axle
Steering	Marles

Body details

Overall height	14′ $3\frac{1}{4}″$		*Overall width*	7′ 6″
Seating, outside	30		*Seating, outside*	26
Unladen weight	6 tons 13 cwt.		*Laden weight*	10 tons 9 cwt.

Vehicles built

STD1–90 Leyland all-metal body. Clash transmission
STD91–100 Leyland all-metal body. Lysholm·Smith torque convertor.

(*Below*) Nearside view of STD.

25 **10T Type** 1938

1938 SAW THE entry to service of a second generation of Green Line coaches. Although it still retained the T classification it could be regarded as a development of the 9T9 from two years earlier. The power from the engine had been found lacking so the 8·8 litre oil engine was utilised instead of the STL 7·7 litre. Braking was improved by fitting a bigger servo motor compared with the 9T9.

The body was of Chiswick construction and had an improved appearance by the absence of the hump effect of the 9T9. The majority were allocated as coaches though a few were used as country buses. Many were converted to ambulances during the second World War.

In order to climb Titsey Hill a few were fitted with a revised differential ratio of 6¼:1 instead of 5½:1 with a revised low ratio gearbox.

All were withdrawn as coaches and in 1951/52 some vehicles were painted red and used as buses in the Central area.

Chassis details MAKER'S REF: A.E.C. 0662 SERIES

Overall length	27' 5"	*Rear axle*	Fully floating worm gear, 5½:1 *
Wheelbase	17' 0"	*Gearbox*	Pre-selective 4-speed
Frame	Channel	*Clutch*	Fluid flywheel
Front axle	I section taper roller bearings		
Engine	A.E.C. 180 type, 90 bhp, 6-cylinder oil, 8·8 litres, 115 mm bore, 142 mm. stroke		
Suspension	Leaf springs with shock absorbers		
Brakes	Lockheed servo	*Steering*	A.E.C. worm-and-nut
Turning circle	59' 0"		

* A small number were altered to 6¼:1 for Titsey Hill operation.

Body details

COACH

Overall height	10' 1½"	*Overall width*	7' 4" (over pillars)	*Unladen weight*	6 tons 12 cwt.
Seating, coach	30	*Seating, bus*	34	*Laden weight*	8 tons 15 cwt.

Vehicles built

T453–718 (total 226). Chiswick-built bodies, country buses or coaches

(*Below*) 10T10 Green Line coach, the last of the great pre-war T class.

26 LTC Type 1937

In order to cope with private hire, L.P.T.B. placed orders for 24 coaches based on the LT chassis utilising petrol engines withdrawn from the LT class when oil engines were fitted to those vehicles. They entered service in 1937.

The body by Weymann was not unlike a 'stretched' version of the 10T10 design but with twin axles at the rear. In 1948/49 oil engines were fitted from scrapped LT buses.

As an improvement three of the vehicles were fitted with cant glasses in the roof to make them into observation coaches.

In 1952 all 24 vehicles were withdrawn from service.

Chassis details MAKER'S REF: A.E.C. 663 SERIES

Front axle	I section	*Gearbox*	Pre-selective gearbox
Rear axle	Fully floating 6¾":1 worm	*Clutch*	Fluid flywheel
Engine	A.E.C. A145 petrol. 8·8 litres, 110 mm. bore, 130 mm. stroke. ex LT		
Suspension	Leaf-spring shock absorbers front		
Brakes	Lockheed servo		

Body details

Seating capacity 32
Unladen weight 8 tons 2 cwt.   *Laden weight* 10 tons 5 cwt.

Vehicles built

LTC1–24 Weymann body. Converted to Oil Engine 1949. 3 bodies modified with cant roof glasses.

(*Below*) Private Hire L.T.C. coach, a vehicle based on the LT petrol-engined chassis. It was useful as it carried large loads, and the seating, with Private Hire in mind, was with extra-large well-upholstered seats. The recess in the centre of the offside of the body is to carry tour boards.

27 TF Type 1939

This was an advanced vehicle and could be claimed to be the first to be fitted with an engine designed for underfloor mounting. The chassis design was made of channel members presenting a flat surface throughout its length to which the body was rigidly attached at outriggers, forming an integral arrangement. The driver was placed in his normal cab, entry being through a door in the front of the saloon. With the engine underfloor, the visibility from the driving seat was to a standard still to be equalled.

Although the experimental or prototype which appeared in 1937 was fitted with different external types of cab from time to time, by the time production started in 1939 a much more pleasing style had been evolved, one of the most attractive pre-war designs.

The first 12 bodies were by Park Royal and these vehicles formed part of the private hire fleet. Windows were incorporated at the cant rail to give better visibility.

The bulk of the fleet, (TF14–88) formed an essential part of the Green Line fleet operating from Romford and Grays. The second World War intervened and severely reduced their working life on Green Line services as most were withdrawn for conversion to ambulances. The private hire vehicles were almost all destroyed by enemy action at Bull Yard, Peckham. Only one (TF9) survived.

After the war the coaches were gradually returned to service as the Green Line services were reinstated, but it became difficult to obtain spares for such a small build of vehicle, which, it must be admitted, was years ahead of its time.

As the RF vehicles appeared the TF was transferred to Country Bus duty for a short time before being sold.

Chassis details MAKER'S REF: LEYLAND F.E.C.

Track	Front 6′ 3″, rear 5′ 8½″
Overall length	27′ 6″
Wheelbase	18′ 5″
Frame	Channel flat throughout length
Front axle	Leyland 6 type
Rear axle	Worm gear 5·2:1
Gearbox	A.E.C. pre-selective air pressure (reverse to 3RT)
Clutch	A.E.C. fluid flywheel
Engine	Leyland 6-cylinder oil, 8·6 litre flat. Bore 4½″, stroke 5½″. 58 bhp at 1000 rpm
Suspension	Leaf springs
Brakes	Air pressure
Steering	A.E.C. worm-and-nut

Body details

Overall height	9′ 10 3/16″	*Overall width*	7′ 5½″
Seating, coach	33	*Seating, bus*	34

COACH

Unladen weight	6 tons 11 cwt.	*Laden weight*	8 tons 19 cwt.

Vehicles built

TF 1 Prototype (1937)
2-13 Private Hire 33 seats. P.R.V. body (1939)
14-88 Green Line Coach 34 seats. Chiswick body (1939)

(*Above*) Prototype TF1. An advanced bus or coach giving a driver vision never equalled in later vehicles. This vehicle was first used on the Tunbridge Wells Green Line route, then it ran as a Private Hire coach, and was later sold. Strangely, it was hired back to London Transport to help with the grave vehicle shortage after the second World War and ran, as a bus in peak hours. This view is in Bushey Park.

(*Below*) Production batch TF with Chiswick-built body.
(*Right*) Private Hire TF, with P.R.V. body. Note the early radio-aerial in the forward part of the coach, and the curved glass panels in the side roof that earned these coaches the nickname of 'glasshouses'. Many of these advanced coaches were destroyed by bombing, at Peckham, during the second World War.

28 **RT Type** 1939

N THE LATE part of the 1930s the newer STL vehicles had been used for experimentation with transmissions, automatic chassis lubrication, rubber-mounted engines on the chassis and metal body construction. This all culminated in the new A.E.C. Regent Mark III.

In order to test under road conditions, a prototype chassis was fitted with an open staircase body removed from one of the independently acquired Leyland 'TD' vehicles and was given the bonnet number ST1140. Eventually it received a Chiswick body and became RT1. Then followed a build of 150, all with Chiswick bodies. Further building ceased because of the second World War and after a time, shortage of spares forced the vehicles to be taken out of service.

The history of some of the buses makes interesting reading. RT19 was painted green and loaned to many provincial operators as part of an A.E.C. sales promotion. By 1942 it had been painted red and joined its fellow buses at Putney Bridge (F) and Chelverton Road (AF). Later after the war, the chassis of this vehicle was sent to A.E.C. when a resumption of bus production was contemplated. After some improvements had been made, it received the body from RT1, whose chassis by this time had been scrapped.

RT97 was badly damaged during the war and it was converted to a pay-as-you-board vehicle for central area operation. This proved unsuccessful and after a short period as a Green Line coach on Route 721 it was used for developing a double-deck coach which emerged in 1949 as RTC1. Eventually relegated to Country bus work, it was then withdrawn for heating development trials at Chiswick. Ultimately it was sold out of service.

By 1955 the delivery of the post-war RT enabled these early vehicles to be relegated to 'trainer' duties with the exception of a few which were painted green and allocated to Hertford (HG) to cover a route which operated over a weight-restricted bridge.

Chassis details MAKER'S REF: 0961

Track	Front 6' 3$\frac{9}{16}$", rear 5' 9$\frac{1}{2}$"
Overall length	26' 0"
Wheelbase	16' 4"
Frame	Channel section
Front axle	I section taper roller bearings
Rear axle	Worm gear, 5$\frac{3}{4}$:1, fully floating parallel bearings
Gearbox	Air pressure operated, pre-selective 4-speed
Clutch	Fluid flywheel
Engine	A.E.C. 185 6-cylinder oil, 9·6 litre, 120 mm. bore, 142 mm. stroke, 100 bhp
Suspension	Leaf springs
Brakes	Air pressure
Steering	A.E.C. worm-and-nut *Turning circle* 59' 0"

Modifications were made at a later date to dynamo drive, compressor type and drive leading to creation of different chassis sub-codes.

Body details

Overall width	7' 6"	
Seating, inside	26	*Seating, outside* 30
Unladen weight	6 tons 10 cwt 2 qtrs 14lbs (1/2RT2/1)	*Laden weight* 10 tons

Vehicles built

RT1 Prototype but fitted with open stair body—ST1140
RT2–151 Production vehicles

(*Below*) The mysterious 'ugly duckling'. The first RT chassis was bodied with an ancient ST body for evaluation trials. It did run on Route 18, but was often to be seen in the streets of Putney where, in due course, the first production RTs were allocated to Chelverton Road and Putney Bridge garages. (*Top Right*) The bus transformed! It is February 1939 and the first modern RT body appears on a bus in London. The chassis used is the one in the previous photograph. It ran on Route 22, not 164A.

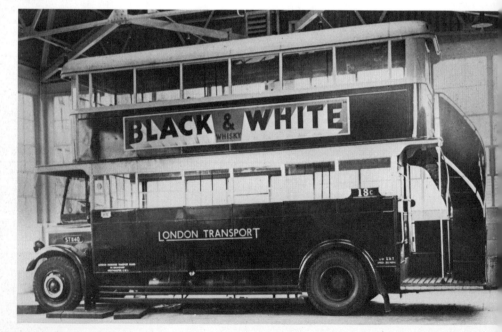

(*Left*) RT97, reconstructed at Chiswick for another Pay-as-you-enter experiment; with a rear-end pay booth and NCR issuing machine. This bus, was later fitted with standard body and, after rebodying, it became a double-deck coach.

AS AN ATTEMPT to produce an economical one-man 20-seater bus, both London Transport and Leyland Motors combined in 1939 to produce a rear engined vehicle but having a body much similar to the TF Green Line coach. By employing a rear engine as opposed to the underfloor of the TF, it was possible to have the overall height lower by 1' as well as a similar floor line to ease boarding and alighting. A sideways or transverse mounted engine was used behind the rear axle driving through a 4-speed gearbox with differential and right angle drive to a De Dion rear axle.

Forty-nine of these attractive vehicles were built in 1939/40, but as the war intensified it curtailed further production. They ran in the Central area until shortage of spares led to their withdrawal and they were stored at Reigate and Slough. The CR buses reappeared in 1946, acting as relief vehicles in Central areas, and for the Olympic Games in 1948. Finally six reappeared in the Country area running from Epping, East Grinstead and Tring in 1952. With the introduction of the GS in 1953 these remaining vehicles were withdrawn.

It is said that the war prevented the development of this revolutionary vehicle which could have altered the pattern of small bus design.

Chassis details MAKER'S REF: LEYLAND CUB R.E.C.

Overall length	22' 6"
Wheelbase	14' 9"
Frame	Channel section
Front axle	H section
Rear axle*	Taper roller, 5·5:1 ratio
Gearbox*	Special Leyland 4-speed clash
Clutch	Dry plate
Engine	Leyland E141 4·37 litres, bore 3½", stroke 5", 34 bhp at 1000 rpm
Suspension	Leaf springs
Brakes	Girling wedge two leading shoe. Lockheed master cylinder
Steering	Worm-and-nut
Turning circle	56'

Combined installation – see text.

Body details

Overall height	8' 10½"	Overall width	7' 4½" (over pillars)
Seating	20		

Vehicles built

CR1–49 Chiswick bodies

Top Left) RT97, modified as Green Line Coach RTC1. Fire and overheating seemed to overshadow this particular bus; on another occasion it was found overheating owing to defective passenger heating switches whilst in service, but was withdrawn that day before the damage was serious.

Bottom Left) One of the advanced CR buses; this one working the Kingston routes. Pay-as-you-enter conditions applied. This bus is in wartime dress, with protective illumination.

30 **STD Type** 1942

WITH THE OUTBREAK of war in 1939 only a few manufacturers were allowed to continu
with bus chassis manufacturing. The Leyland organization was committed to othe
work, but were allowed to finish the chassis already being built. Hence London Transpor
received 11 of the TD7 class which was really an extension of the previous 'Hendon' STI
but with iron and steel substituted for the alloy parts. These vehicles were fitted with a
austerity body by Park Royal and entered service in 1942 and were allocated to Victori
(GM).

Chassis details MAKER'S REF: LEYLAND TD7

Front axle	Alloy steel forging taper roller bearings
Rear axle	Fully floating worm axle 5·4:1
Gearbox	4 speed constant mesh silent third
Clutch	Single plate dry plate
Engine	6 cylinder oil 58 bhp at 1000 rpm $4\frac{1}{2}''$ bore $\times$ $5\frac{1}{2}''$ stroke
Suspension	Leaf springs with anchor plates with arm type shock absorbers
Brakes	Triple servo automatic adjusters
Steering	Worm-and-nut

Body details

Seating capacity inside 26, outside 30
Unladen weight 6 tons 19 cwt.   *Laden weight* 10 tons 15 cwt.

Vehicles built

STD 101–111 P.R.V. body

(*Below*) Wartime STD bus, one of a small batch unfrozen and released to London Transport in
1942. Note the completeness of the anti-blast netting, with only the lower half of the front window
unobscured and tiny viewing apertures.

31 B Type 1942

BRISTOL TRAMWAYS and Carriage Co. was one of the few companies permitted to carry on bus construction during the war. It was inevitable that London Transport would sooner or later receive an allocation of these wartime buses. In 1942 the first nine to be allocated were fitted with a Gardner 5-cylinder engine with a fairly high radiator and bonnet line, and were allocated to Hanwell Garage to operate on Route 97. They were known as Bristol K5G and were built to a Ministry of Supply specification.

Three years later a further allocation of 20 Bristol vehicles was made, these being Bristol K6A with A.E.C. 7·7 litre engines. The body by Duple was far less austere and had upholstered seats compared with the wooden seats fitted in the first nine. These vehicles were again allocated to Hanwell for the 83/92/92A services.

In the interests of standardization, in 1949 the Gardner engines from the K5G were replaced by A.E.C. 7·7 to release them as spares for the Guy Arabs, which used the Gardner 5-cylinder.

In 1953 the K6A were sold out of service to other operators such as Brighton Hove & District and in some cases were given an extra lease of life by fitting new E.C.W. bodies at a later date.

Attention is drawn to the 180 Bristol K type borrowed from the Tilling Companies as detailed in Chapter 39.

Below) First batch of wartime Bristol K5G, coded B. Their ponderous manual gearboxes contrasted badly with the flexible drive of pre-war London buses.

Chassis details MAKER'S REF: BRISTOL K

Track	Front 6' 4½", rear 5' 10"
Overall length	25' 11"
Wheelbase	16' 3"
Frame	Channel section
Front axle	Taper roller 1 section beam
Rear axle	Fully floating worm 6·0:1 roller bearing
Gearbox	4 speed clash
Clutch	16" diameter single plate dry
Engine	B 1–9 Gardner 5LW(later converted to A.E.C. A202) 10–29 A.E.C. 7·7 litre A202
Suspension	Leaf springs shock absorbers
Brakes	Triple servo
Steering	Worm-and-quadrant (Marles type)
Turning circle	59' 0"

Body details

Overall height 14' 6"	*Unladen weight*
Overall width 7' 6"	(1–9) 7 tons 0 cwt. (10–29) 7 tons 3 cwt.
Seating capacity	*Laden weight*
inside 26, outside 30	(1–9) 10 tons 13 cwt. (10–29) 10 tons 13 cwt.

Vehicles built

1B 1–9 K5G Gardner 5LW engine (later changed to A.E.C. 7·7) Park Royal body
2B 10–19 K6A A.E.C. 7·7 litre engine Duple body

(*Below*) A bus from the second batch of B type buses, in service in Greenford Road at the Iron Bridge.   *J. Higham*

32 **G Type** 1942

GUY MOTORS of Wolverhampton was the second supplier of bus chassis during the war years, the third being Daimler. Bus chassis production had ceased at Fallings Park, Wolverhampton, some six years before the war, and it was very strange that Guys should be chosen to start again.

All the chassis were fitted with the Gardner engine, dry plate clutch and constant mesh gearbox. Although provision was made for fitting the 6-cylinder Gardners on later deliveries by carrying the radiator forward, all those allocated to London were actually fitted with the 5-cylinder version because of the fairly flat terrain over which they operated.

At first the bodies were very austere but were fitted with upholstered seats. These first vehicles were built by Park Royal and Weymann with an odd one later by Duple. Then slatted seats were introduced, to give way later to upholstered seats again. It was not until the Northern Counties bodies appeared with the curved front end to the top deck and the pronounced sweep to the roof at the rear that a break with wartime austerity was noticed.

(*Below*) A Guy Arab bus in grey delivery paint, with P.R.V. body, before fitment of side destination box.

By the end of the programme the bodies were by no less than five body builders of which many were to fairly austere M.O.S. requirements. On the other hand the chassis contained very few variations from its original inception.

Thirty-four vehicles (G269–311, 319–357 and 431–453) were fitted with single plate clutch and constant mesh gearbox.

Delivery of the first 31 Guys with Park Royal bodies commenced in December 1942. The body of G30 was destroyed by enemy action and replaced in June 1944 by one built by Northern Coach Builders.

Eighteen bodies by Weymann (G32–42, 44–50) arrived early in 1943. G43, new in July 1943, was a 'one off' body by Duple. G51–136 were supplied by Park Royal during 1943/4. Weymann supplied some more bodies in 1945 these being fitted to G137/8, 369–430. Further Park Royal deliveries arrived during 1945, these being G139–153, 194–218, 319–357, 431–435.

Northern Counties provided the more pleasant all-metal bodies for G154–173, 219–257, 269–311. The last body builder, who supplied rather angular style bodies for the Guys, was Massey. The 49 buses were G174–193, 258–268, 312–318 and 358–368.

The first forty Guys went to Tottenham for route 76, later deliveries went to Southall, Alperton, Enfield and a number of East London garages including Upton Park, Barking and Hornchurch.

By 1951 the bodies on these vehicles were beginning to show signs of wear and tear and the vehicles did not match up to the standard of the RT which was then coming into service in large quantities; so it was decided to withdraw them from service. Many were sold to overseas buyers and so took on a second life.

Chassis details MAKER'S REF: GUY ARAB

Track	Front 6′ 3⅞″, rear 5′ 10″
Wheelbase	16′ 3″
Rear axle	Fully floating taper roller worm 5·6 ratio
Gearbox	Constant mesh 3rd—4 speed box
Clutch	Double plate clutch 15⅞″ diameter.
Engine	Gardner 5LW 5 cylinder oil E5675 85 hp at 1700 rpm 4¼″ 6″ stroke
Suspension	Semi elliptical leaf springs with shock absorbers
Brakes	Lockheed servo assisted
Steering	Marles cam-and-double roller
Turning circle	60′

Body details

Seating
  inside 26, outside 30

Unladen weight
  7 tons 12 cwt. (2G2)
Laden weight
  11 tons 5 cwt.

Vehicles built

G 1– 29	Park Royal body. 35 gallon fuel tank fitted instead of 28—(10 vehicles)
30	Northern Coachbuilders. Original P.R.V. body destroyed
31– 50	Weymann
(except 43 Duple)	
51–136	P.R.V. Front end extended to fit Gardner 6LW engine if required. 12V systems. New style front wings
137–138	Weymann
139–153	P.R.V. Upholstered seats radiussed roof door
154–173	Northern Counties
174–193	Massey
194–218	P.R.V.
219–257	Northern Counties
258–268	Massey
269–311	Northern Counties. (34 vehicles were fitted with single plate clutch and constant mesh gearbox)
312–318	Massey ·
319–357	P.R.V.
358–368	Massey
369–398	Weymann
399–409	Weymann
410–430	Weymann
431–435	P.R.V.

Note: G436 was a Guy version of the 'RT' type of vehicle, employing a Meadows 10·8 litre engines, fluid flywheel, preselector gearbox and air pressure brakes. It carried a P.R.V. all metal body and was purchased in 1950 and ran from Nunhead (AH) and Old Kent Road (P) on Route 173 until transferred to Enfield (E) to work on Route 121. Sold to Yugoslavia in 1954.

Left) Guy G13.

(*Above*) The 'odd Guy'. G30, rebodied
by Northern Coachworks.

Alan B. Cross

(*Right*) Guy with Massey coachwork
at Royal Forest Hotel, Chingford. It is
in late wartime livery.

33 **D Type** 1944

TRANSPORT VEHICLES (DAIMLER) COVENTRY were one of the firms allowed to continue building bus chassis during the war. The Daimler chassis, apart from the DST in 1930, had not previously been in London service and they still employed the pre-selective gearbox and fluid flywheel long pioneered by this company. The chassis was a continuation of that built immediately before the war, but the Gardner engine had given way to the A.E.C. 7·7 litre, well known to London in the STL family. Because of this build they were classified CWA6 with the 'A' standing for A.E.C., as opposed to the code COG5 given to the Gardner.

(*Above*) Lowbridge Daimler, with Duple body. You can see the varnished slatted seats that early wartime buses carried. The standard diamond viewing ports in the netting are similiar to that provided on Underground trains of the time, and should be compared with that shown in illustration of the STD bus on page 94. This bus ran on Route 127, which passed under the low bridge at Worcester Park Station.

(*Left*) Duple-bodied D23 one of many running from Merton Garage.

The first vehicles in 1944 had austerity bodies with the first six by Duple with a low-bridge body operation on Bus 127 from Merton Garage followed by 28 highbridge. Production switched to Brush at 35 with a highbridge body, reverting to Duples when No. 74 was reached. These still had highbridge bodies. This continued to No. 92 when production reverted to Brush. Body production remained with Brush until 127, but certain minor differences existed.

D127 was fitted with a Daimler 8·6 litre oil engine as an experiment to be followed later by a further 11 known as CWD6.

These vehicles spent their entire life at Merton Garage except for 37 painted in Green Line livery for operation of the Aldgate services from Romford (London Road) replacing the elderly STL vehicles. Later they were painted red and transferred to Merton.

With the introduction of Park Royal as body supplier at D182 in 1946, the bodies took a more peacetime look and this continued to the final vehicle at D281. These 100 buses formed the backbone of the services from Sutton. Apart from the batch of 12 Daimler engines, the chassis was otherwise unaltered.

After service in London many vehicles had a further lease of life with Belfast Corporation.

Chassis details MAKER'S REF: DAIMLER CWA 6/CWD 6

Track	Front 6' 6⅛", rear 5' 10¼"
Overall length	25' 11"
Wheelbase	16' 3 5/32"
Frame	Channel
Front axle	H section. Taper roller
Rear axle	Fully floating taper roller worm gear 5¾:1
Gearbox	4 speed pre-selective
Clutch	Fluid flywheel
Engine	A.E.C. 7·7 litre A 173 105 mm. bore, 146 mm. stroke 95 bhp at 1750 rpm
Suspension	Semi elliptical leaf
Brakes	Lockheed servo asissted
Steering	Worm-and-nut
Turning circle	59'

Body details

Overall width 7' 6"
Seating
inside 26, outside 30

Unladen weight
7 tons 4 cwt. (1.D.1)
Laden weight
10 tons 19 cwt. (1.D.1)

Vehicles built

D	1– 6	Duple lowbridge body. (55 seats, 28 out 27 in)
	7– 34	Duple highbridge body. (56 seats, 30 out 26 in)
	35– 61	Brush highbridge body
	62– 73	Brush highbridge body
	74– 92	Duple highbridge body
	93–115	Brush highbridge body. Radiussed rear roof dome
	116–126	Brush highbridge body
	127	Brush highbridge body. Daimler D 1 engine 8·6 litre
	128–131	Duple lowbridge body. (55 seats as 1–6)
	132–181	Duple highbridge body. (12 with Daimler engines—127, 138, 139, 140, 142, 150, 155, 160, 162, 171, 180 and 181)
	182–281	Park Royal highbridge body

(*Left*) Duple-bodied Daimler for Green Line work. This coach is on Express 722, and seen here at Minories lay-by, Aldgate.

(*Below*) Daimler with P.R.V. Body. All of these buses worked from Sutton Garage.

34 STL & T Types 1945, 1946

In order to reduce the vehicle shortage in London, 20 double-deckers were purchased from A.E.C. in 1945 and numbered STL2682–2701, it being their first production after the war. The chassis differed very little from that of the 'unfrozen' STLs purchased in 1942 (2648–2681). The body, by Weymann, showed a departure from wartime austerity by the curved outward panel at the skirt which was the characteristic of this builder. Because of their clash type gearboxes and plate clutches they were finally allocated to the country area working from Watford (High Street) and Luton on Routes 321 and 351.

To help the aging single-deck fleet, 50 single-deck versions were purchased in 1946 and fitted with a body again by Weymann. The outward sweep of the body was retained but sliding windows were fitted. The radiator was deeper, as on the STL type, which clearly identified the post-war production of A.E.C.

The single-deckers were painted red and allocated to Kingston and Uxbridge. They were withdrawn in November 1958.

Chassis details MAKER'S REF: 18 STL 20—A.E.C. 0661 & 14 T 12—A.E.C. 0662

Track
Overall length 18 STL—25' 11⅝" 14 T—27' 4½"
Wheelbase 18 STL—16' 4" 14 T—17' 6"
Frame Channel
Front axle I section taper roller bearings
Rear axle Worm. Fully floating
Gearbox Clash
Clutch Single plate
Engine A.E.C. 7·7 litre A 173
Suspension Leaf springs
Brakes Triple servo
Steering Worm-and-nut
Turning circle 59' 0"

Body details

18 STL
Overall width 7' 5⅝"   *Seating* 56
Unladen weight 6 tons 0 cwt.   *Laden weight* 8 tons 8 cwt.
14 T
Overall height 9' 4¼"   *Overall width* 7' 5½"
Seating 35 (33 from 1949)   *Laden weight* 11 tons 18 cwt.
Unladen weight 7 tons 0 cwt.

Vehicles built

18 STL   STL 2682–2701. Weymann body. 56 seats
14 T   T 719–768. Weymann body. 33 seats

(*Top Right*) An STL from the immediate post war days (coded for Watford High Street Garage). These lightweight buses were not popular with crews, and the gangways were narrow for fare collection.

(*Bottom Right*) Single-deck Weymann bodied T bus.

35 STD & TD Types 1946

THESE VEHICLES were the post-war equivalent of the earlier Leyland double-deck Titan. The bodywork was, once again, metal construction, built by Leyland, and was fairly standard throughout the country with a few modifications to suit London Transport. However, the engine was of smaller capacity than the earlier STD but the gearbox was still constant mesh with a friction clutch. Braking was by triple vacuum servo.

These vehicles were purchased as a temporary measure in 1946 until the RT began to arrive in September 1947. They spent their life in a comparatively small number of garages—Loughton, Hanwell, Croydon and Victoria, and were referred to in Leyland terms as PD1. Comparison of this vehicle with its previous counterpart showed a fairly significant reduction in weight.

In order to strengthen the single-deck fleet, two batches of the single-deck version known as PS1 were purchased. The first 31 were fitted with Weymann bodies. A further 100 were bought with a Mann Egerton body not unlike that fitted to the 15T class. These later vehicles differed from the earlier PD1 and PS1 in that a cast radiator was fitted instead of the chromium shell. These single deckers were not fitted with doors since they were all to operate in the Central area. The vehicles were to bridge the gap until the RF appeared on the scene from 1952 onwards.

Chassis details MAKER'S REF: LEYLAND TITAN PD1 OR PS1

Track	Front 6' 4$\frac{9}{16}$", rear 5' 8·8"
Overal length	25' 11$\frac{1}{8}$"
Wheelbase	16' 3" (TD 17' 6")
Frame	Nickel steel channel
Front axle	H section beam taper roller
Rear axle	Fully floating underslung worm 5·4:1 (TD 4·8:1)
Gearbox	4 speed constant mesh
Clutch	Single plate 16$\frac{1}{4}$" diameter
Engine	7·4 litre Leyland oil E 181/4 4$\frac{3}{8}$" bore 5" stroke 100 bhp at 1800 rpm
Suspension	Leaf springs with shock absorbers
Brakes	Triple servo
Steering	Marles cam-and-double roller
Turning circle	60'

Body details

STD

Overall height 14' 4$\frac{7}{8}$"	*Overall width* 7' 4"
Seating outside 30	*Seating* inside 26
Unladen weight 7 tons 5 cwt.	*Laden weight* 10 tons 17 cwt.

TD

Seating (Weymann body) 33	*Seating* (Mann Egerton) 31/30
Unladen weight 6 tons 2 cwt.	*Laden weight* 8 tons 9 cwt.

Vehicles built

Double-Deck	STD 112–176. All metal Leyland body
Single-Deck	TD 1–31. Weymann body
Single-Deck	TD 32–131. Mann Egerton body

(*Above*) Standard STD bus from the post-war days.

(*Left*) Single-deck TD; first post-war delivery.

(*Above*) Mann Egerton-bodied TD.

(*Below*) Mobile Training Unit carried on a RT chassis. After the war, as RT production batches appeared, a heavy training programme was implemented at many London garages which were to receive them.

36 **RT Type** 1947

THE SECOND World War halted production of the 2RT. It was natural, afterwards, to take a further look at the 2RT and apply any lessons that had been learnt from its somewhat limited service operation, and incorporate any techniques that had been developed during the war.

London Transport had been involved in the manufacture of Handley Page Halifax aircraft at Chiswick, and at its Aldenham Depot (originally planned as a railway depot for an abortive extension of the Northern Line). Starting with the basic 2RT idea, RT19 was chosen to carry out chassis modifications to modernize it, and the body was transferred to RT52. A new design of body was evolved which could be built on a mass production line with all components jig-built to ensure full interchangeability. The attachment of the body to the chassis was at four points which could be guaranteed on all vehicles and the bodies could be interchanged. This was to be advantageous at vehicle overhaul (when the body overhaul takes longer than the chassis), so each body did not hold up the production line to wait for its own chassis again.

Although externally there did not appear to be much difference between the pre-war and post-war bodies, there was quite a large absence of timber in the 3RT. To counteract rear end accidents which often led to distortion of the chassis side members, these members were cut short immediately behind the rear axle. To assist body repair, the whole staircase unit was detachable. Improvements had also been made in the mechanical components such as air pressure system, fluid flywheel, gearbox and rear axle. A.E.C. were entrusted with the chassis contract and production commenced in 1947. Body contracts went to Park Royal and Weymann, starting two distinct bonnet number series.

In order to obtain more bodies to meet the flow of chassis from A.E.C., two other body-builders were invited to supply. The first of these, Saunders Roe of Anglesey, built a body very similar to the external appearance of the PRV/Weymann body but utilising their own construction. The other supplier was Cravens, but these bodies were less similar. The apparent difference was an additional 5th window compared with the four lower deck windows of other builders. The Craven vehicles were kept under one series RT1402–1521 whereas the Saunders were given RT1152–1401 and 4218–4267.

Production then reverted to the two main suppliers until RT4396 when it became evident these bodies were outstepping chassis production and it was decided to re-build the later STL class. The bodies were taken from STL2516–2647 and fitted to the earlier 4/9STL whose bodies (in particular the PRV-STL2014–2188) were rather the worse for wear. The chassis was completely stripped and reworked to take a production Park Royal body. Although outwardly similar, they retained the somewhat smaller STL 7·7 litre engine and pre-selective gearbox and were restricted to flat terrain because of the poorer power/weight ratio compared to the 3RT. They were easily recognised by their pre-war FJJ and FXT registrations and their SRT bonnet letters. Although earlier chassis were later included, the build ceased at SRT160. A place in the RT sequence was saved for these vehicles (RT4397–4556) when the correct chassis became available. The full SRT programme was never carried out because A.E.C. were able to supply chassis before the completion of the SRT conversion, as this was called.

From RT4557·4825 production was split between PRV and Weymann.

Throughout the programme bodies were painted red or green according to traffic requirements and at later dates there was some interchange of colours. Other than this there was little obvious variation apart from the 57 (36 by Weymann, 21 by PRV) for the Aldgate series of Green Line routes.

The RT class probably represents the largest number of vehicles with only minor modifications in design and could be claimed to be a major step forward in public service design after the war. By the time the RT is withdrawn from service in the late seventies it will have served London for some 30 years.

Chassis details MAKER'S REF: A.E.C. 0961/1

Track	Front 6' 3½", rear 5' 9 3/16"
Overall length	21' 9 11/32" (chassis is tail less)
Wheelbase	16' 4"
Frame	Channel
Front axle	Reversed Elliot taper roller bearings
Rear axle	Worm gear 5·1/6:1 fully floating parallel bearings
Gearbox	A.E.C. air-pressure-operated pre-selective 4 speed
Clutch	18" fluid flywheel
Engine	A.E.C. A 204 6 cylinder oil 120 mm. bore, 142 mm. stroke 115 bhp at 1800 rpm
Suspension	Leaf springs
Brakes	Air pressure
Steering	A.E.C. worm-and-nut
Turning circle	57' 1"

Body details

Overall height 14' 3¾"
Overall width 7' 5½"
Seating
inside 26, outside 30

Unladen weight
7 tons 5 cwt.
Laden weight
11 tons 0 cwt.

Vehicles built

RT 152– 401	Park Royal body
402– 651	Weymann body
652– 961	P.R.V. body
962–1151	Weymann body
1152–1401	Saunders body
1402–1521	Craven body. (Additional window on each side)
1522–2121	P.R.V. body
2122–2521	Weymann body
2522–2655	P.R.V. body
2656–2774	Weymann body
2775–3041	P.R.V. body
3042–4217	Weymann body
4218–4267	Saunders body
4268–4396	P.R.V. body
4397–4446	P.R.V. body. (Bodies originally fitted to rebuild STL—bonnet letter SRT)
4447–4556	P.R.V. body
4557–4568	Weymann body
4569–4684	P.R.V. body
4685–4794	Weymann body
4795–4825	P.R.V. body

(*Top Right*) RT1155, a Saunders-Roe Body. These well-built buses were rather heavier than normal buses.

(*Bottom Right*) A Craven body on a 3RT chassis, allocated to London Transport's Country area. This was another well-built but heavy body, and these buses were sold out of service to independent operators such as 'Red Rover' of Aylesbury, where they ran successfully for many years.

(*Right*) Green Line coach for the Aldgate services. No coaches carried advertisements in the days when they formed part of the London Transport fleet.

(*Below*) The SRT; an STL conversion with Palmers Green codes. It was under-engined and disliked by crews.

37 **RTL & RTW Types** 1948

AS THE Associated Equipment Company did not have the production capacity to meet the replacement rate of the London Transport fleet, agreement was reached between London Transport and A.E.C. for Leyland to build a considerable number of chassis.

The first stipulation was that the chassis must be able to take the standard 'RT' body without serious alteration. Within this restriction Leyland offered their standard PD2 type steering, front and rear axles, revised 0600 engine, but the transmission was to be supplied by A.E.C.

A prototype vehicle was delivered in May 1948 and fitted with a Park Royal body with 'lighthouse' route number box, and was numbered curiously RTL501. The addition of the 'L' in the bonnet number had previously indicated a lengthened chassis but on this occasion it was to signify RT Leyland or as it was more often referred to as 'Leyland RT'. The use of 501 was to allow for 500 Leyland RT which were to be 8′ 0″ wide as opposed to previous vehicles being 7′ 6″. It was soon realised that to include two different widths of chassis in one bonnet code could present difficulties with the operating staff and before deliveries of the wider vehicles commenced they were given the letters RTW, the W representing 'wide'.

After service running at Turnham Green, production vehicles started to appear in December 1948 with bodies in the first place from M.C.W. However, delays ensued and Park Royal supplied the bodies for the first 550, with M.C.W. doing only 450.

(*Below*) The first 8 foot-wide bus the RTW. It was later moved to routes running through the West End to see how the wider bus would fare with congested traffic.

Further deliveries were received up to RTL1468 of which all but one were Park Royal. Because of service difficulties with front end vibrations it was decided to experiment with RTL1337 to test out various modifications. When these tests were completed RTL 1337 was registered with an RT series number plate. The final batch of vehicles 1469–1631 having been built as standard were converted to the revised arrangements by the service depot of Leyland Motors then at Borehamwood before entering service.

The 500 wide buses carried a Leyland-built all-metal body which closely resembled the RT appearance. The chassis was of normal width with a widened front axle. In the case of the rear axle the extra six inches was gained by extended hubs. The idea behind this was to test whether an 8' 0" wide vehicle presented any problems and as a start they were allocated to outer London routes. Later in their service life tests were constructed using these buses on routes that converged on Piccadilly Circus and Kensington High Street. Delivery was made commencing April 1948 all being withdrawn by 1966.

Chassis details MAKER'S REF: 6 AND 7RT PD2/1

Track	Front RTL 6' 3", RTW 6' 9", rear RTL 5' 8", RTW 5' 11½"
Overall length	21' 9 11/32" (tailess)
Wheelbase	16' 4"
Frame	Nickel steel channel
Front axle	H section beam
Rear axle	Worm gear 5·4:1 fully floating taper roller bearings
Gearbox	A.E.C. air pressure operated pre-selective 4 speed
Clutch	A.E.C. 18" fluid flywheel
Engine	Leyland 0600 9·8 litre 115 bhp at 1800 rpm 4·8" bore × 5½" stroke
Suspension	Leaf springs with torsion stabiliser rears
Brakes	Air pressure
Steering	Marles cam-and-roller
Turning circle	RTL 58' 3"
	RTW 56' 0"

Body details

RTL
Overall height 14' 4"	*Overall width* 7' 6"
Overall length 25' 11"	
Unladen weight 7 tons 19 cwt.	*Laden weight* 11 tons 12 cwt.

RTW
Overall height 14' 4"	*Overall width* 8' 0""
Overall length 25' 11"	
Unladen weight 8 tons 3 cwt.	*Laden weight* 11 tons 16 cwt.

Seating (RTL & RTW) inside 30, outside 26

Vehicles built

RTW	1–500	8' wide Leyland body
RTL	1–550	7' 6" wide P.R.V. body
	551–1000	7' 6" wide M.C.W. body
	1001–1306	7' 6" wide P.R.V. body
	1307	7' 6" wide Weymann body
	1308–1468	7' 6" wide P.R.V. body
	1469–1631	7' 6" wide P.R.V. body (Revised front end chassis)

Notes: 1. The prototype RTL was numbered as RTL501 as it was intended to use RTL1–500 for the 8' 0" wide vehicles and registered as JXC 20.

2. RTL1337 did not enter service until 1954 after engineering use and carried registration OLD 813 out of sequence.

(*Above*) The RTL bus. RTL501 was the prototype Leyland, and was moved to Sidcup on Route 51 after seeing service at Turnham Green Garage on Route 650.

Alan B. Cross

(*Left*) Leyland RT, known as the RTL.

38 T Type 1948

THE WAR YEARS had left the London Transport fleet with a single-deck fleet well above normal age. The Central area had two batches of Leyland Tiger PSI acquired in 1946-8 so for the Country 30 A.E.C. Regals were purchased. By this time the A.E.C. Regent III series of vehicles was well established and the Regal was a single-deck version of the standard A.E.C. Regent. For an order of 30 it was not considered economic to produce a special London Transport variant of this single-decker hence the vehicle chassis had a conventional tail and was not cut off to minimise rear end collision damage. The braking system followed the conventional composite equipment as opposed to the separated units to ease maintenance. Wheel brake assemblies were of somewhat smaller diameter, with thicker drums and greater wheel/drum clearance, a fact which was to be of some consequence when it came to designing the RM in the late 1950s.

A standard body was fitted by Mann Egerton and, in accordance with country practice, a sliding door was fitted. These vehicles spent their whole life in the country bus area.

Chassis details MAKER'S REF: A.E.C. 9621 E

Track	Front 6' 3½", rear 5' 9 3/16 "	*Frame*	Channel
Front axle	Reversed Elliot taper roller bearings		
Rear axle	Worm gear 5·1/6:1 fully floating taper roller bearings		
Gearbox	A.E.C. air pressure operated pre-selective 4 speed		
Clutch	Fluid flywheel		
Engine	A.E.C. A 208 6 cylinder oil 120 mm. bore 142 mm. stroke 115 bhp at 1800 rpm		
Suspension	Leaf springs		
Brakes	Air pressure	*Steering*	A.E.C. worm-and-nut

Body Details

Overall width 7' 6"		*Unladen weight*	6 tons 11 cwt.
Seating 31		*Laden weight*	8 tons 14 cwt.

Vehicles built

T 769–798   Mann Egerton body, Country Bus

(*Left*) A.E.C. Regal standard chassis design: T769 at Chiswick awaiting initial licensing.

116

39 **Bristol K Types** (on loan) 1949

TO EASE THE severe shortage of double-deck buses in London, arrangements were made with the Tilling organization to borrow 200 Bristol 'K' type vehicles in 1949 for a limited period. The vehicles were all new, direct from the bodybuilders painted in the owner's colour scheme but without operator's name. A London Transport roundel, then known as a 'bullseye', was fitted on the radiator. Apart from the carriers for garage letter and running number stencil plates, no other change was made externally to the body. The electrical system was either 12 or 24 volts, according to the owning undertaking.

The vehicles were a mixture of high and lowbridge bodies but whilst the lowbridge buses were useful on a few restricted routes, they were mainly in use with normal height operation.

These vehicles were allocated to a variety of garages, both Central and Country, and were treated as normal vehicles with the exception they did not work on Sundays as there were sufficient London Transport vehicles available.

As new RTs became available the Bristols were delivered to their rightful owner for the first time.

(*Below*) Bristol double-deck owned by Crosville, on hire to London Transport during the bus shortage in the immediate post-war years. This is a lowbridge body and has been given a London Transport 'bullseye' symbol and blinds to make it obvious that it is on stage service for London Transport. *Alan B. Cross*

Chassis details MAKER'S REF: BRISTOL K5G OR K6A

Track	Front 6' 4¾", rear 5' 10"
Overall length	
Wheelbase	16' 3"
Frame	Channel
Front axle	Reverse Elliot 1° camber 2° castor
Rear axle	Underslung worm 6, 6·5 or 5·4:1 according to company
Gearbox	Bristol MS crash
Clutch	Single plate 17" diameter dry
Engine	Gardner 5LW (113 vehicles) 4¼" bore × 6" stroke, 290 lbs. ft. at 1050 rpm 7 litres 85 bhp at 1700 rpm, 13:1 C.R. lbs. ft. A.E.C. A. 173 (87 vehicles) 105 mm. bore × 146 mm. stroke, 294 lbs. ft. at 1000 rpm 7·7 litres 80 bhp at 1650 rpm, 16:1 C.R.
Suspension	Leaf spring, Luvax shock absorbers
Brakes	Vacuum servo
Turning circle	59'
Steering	Marles 21·7 overall ratio

Body details

HIGHBRIDGE
Seating inside 26   *Seating outside* 30
LOWBRIDGE
Seating inside 28   *Seating outside* 27

Vehicles hired

Lowbridge body   156.   Highbridge   44

(*Below*) Highbridge Bristol on loan from Brighton, Hove & District. It carries plates for Tottenham Garage, but has yet to receive blinds. These buses ran on Route 76.   *W. J. Haynes*

40 G Type (RT) 1950

THROUGHOUT the war years the Guy Arab had been one of the pillars of bus transport and it was only to be expected that opportunity would be taken as soon as possible to update this vehicle. The outcome of this was specification ST34 which materialized in the London Transport fleet as G436, the most convenient number in the Guy Arab series.

Technically the bus bore little resemblance to the wartime Arabs in that it had a Meadows 10·35 litre engine with fluid flywheel and preselective gearbox, air-pressure brakes compared with the normal standard of Gardner, clash transmission and Lockheed servo braking. This vehicle was considered as a Guy version of an RT, but in outward appearance there was little resemblance.

The vehicle was allocated first to Old Kent Road (P), then Nunhead (AH) to operate on the Peckham circular service 173 in 1950. After a period it was transferred to Enfield (E) for Route 121, finally being sold out of service overseas.

(*Below*) Prototype Guy RT type bus— given the fleet number G 436.

Chassis details MAKER'S REF: G436 GUY SPECIFICATION ST34

Track	Front 6′ 4⅝″, rear 5′ 10 5/16″
Overall length	25′ 5″
Wheelbase	16′ 3″
Frame	Nickel steel channel
Front axle	H section taper roller
Rear axle	Worm gear 5·6:1 taper roller bearings
Gearbox	4 speed Wilson pre-selective air pressure operated
Clutch	Fluid flywheel
Engine	Meadows 10·35 litre 6 cylinder oil 130 mm. stroke × 130 mm. bore 115 bhp at 1800 rpm
Suspension	Semi-elliptical leaf springs
Brakes	Air pressure operated
Steering	Marles double roller
Turning Circle	60′

Body details

Seating	inside 26, outside 30

Vehicle built

G 436—1 off P.R.V. body

(*Below*) An RLH lowbridge body on a standard A.E.C. chassis—RLH2, on the Amersham services.

41 **RLH Type** 1950

AT THE OUTBREAK OF WAR, London Transport lowbridge fleet consisted of 8 ex-National and Amersham STs, operated on Route 336, and the special 'Godstone' STLs, for working Route 410. Additional lowbridge routes were introduced during the war and resulted in the lowbridge fleet being augmented by the wartime bodies on old STL chassis, for Harrow Weald (Route 230), and Addlestone (Route 436); also the six lowbridge Daimlers from Merton on Route 127. The life of the STs was extended by fitment of oil engines.

With a view to replacement 20 standard A.E.C. Regent Mark III chassis were purchased (often referred to as Provincial RT) and fitted with a lowbridge body by Weymann in 1950. For the number of vehicles involved it was not an economic proposition to adapt to the London 3RT chassis. These vehicles were painted in green livery.

To enable the remainder of the older lowbridge vehicles to be withdrawn a further batch of 56 were ordered in 1952, differing slightly in mechanical specification but still a basic standard A.E.C. chassis. The first 32 were green, and the remainder in red livery.

It has always been the policy not to operate this type of vehicle unless absolutely essential, as the sunken gangway on the offside of the vehicle makes collection of fares rather difficult from bench seats holding 4 people. Wherever possible routes have been altered or the obstructions of railway bridges cleared, either by lifting the bridge or lowering the road. In spite of this, new allocations were opened up for RLH vehicles such as Dalston for 178 and at Reigate for the 447B, but now all have been withdrawn from service, and replaced by single-deckers.

One ex RLH vehicle remains in operation with L.C.B.S. as a mobile clothing store.

Chassis details MAKER'S REF: A.E.C. 9612 E/9613 E

Track	Front 6' 3½", rear 5' 9 3⁄16"
Overall length	25' 11"
Wheelbase	16' 4"
Frame	Channel with tail
Front axle	Reversed Elliot taper roller bearings
Rear axle	Worm gear 5⅛:1 fully floating taper roller bearings
Gearbox	A.E.C. air pressure operated pre-selective 4 speed
Clutch	18" fluid flywheel
Engine	A.E.C. A 6 cylinder oil 120 mm. bore × 142 mm. stroke 115 bhp at 1800 rpm
Suspension	Leaf springs
Brakes	Air pressure
Steering	A.E.C. worm-and-nut
Turning circle	58' 6"

Body details

Overall height 13' 3½"
Overall width 7' 5¾"
Seating
    inside 26, outside 27

Unladen weight
    7 tons 12 cwt.
Laden weight
    11 tons 1 cwt.

Vehicles built

1 RLH   1–20.   Weymann body.   2 RLH   21–76.   Weymann body

42 **Prototypes** (Single Deck) 1949

OTHER THAN THE 30 replacement 15T13 vehicles, the country bus area had not received any new allocation of vehicles. The Green Line fleet was then 14 years old and the design dated from the prewar years. Therefore, two vehicle types were examined for possible consideration of their replacement.

Two vehicles were submitted for consideration: an A.E.C. Regal Mark IV and a Leyland Olympic; both were fitted with an underfloor engine. However, as the Leyland employed a 4-speed constant-mesh gearbox with dry-plate clutch it was decided not to proceed with actual service testing of this vehicle.

The A.E.C. vehicle was then subjected to a series of trials in the country area including St. Albans on Route 355. Eventually UMP 227, as it became known from its registration was found acceptable and from it followed the RF class.

Chassis details MAKER'S REF: VEHICLE TYPE A.E.C. REGAL

Overall length	27′ 6″
Wheelbase	15′ 8½″
Rear axle	Worm 4·4/7:1
Gearbox	Pre-selective
Clutch	Fluid flywheel
Engine	Pilot injection 100 bhp at 1800 rpm
Suspension	Leaf
Brakes	Air pressure manual brake adjustment
Turning circle	61′ 6″ (swept 67′ 11″)
Steering	A.E.C. worm-and-nut

Body details

Overall width	7′ 6″	*Unladen weight*	7 tons 7 cwt.
Seating	40	*Laden weight*	9 tons 17 cwt.

Vehicles built

UMP 227 Park Royal

Chassis details MAKER'S REF: VEHICLE TYPE LEYLAND OLYMPIC

Overall length	28′ 0″
Wheelbase	15′ 7¼″
Rear axle	Spiral bevel 4⅝:1
Gearbox	4 speed constant mesh
Clutch	Dry plate clutch
Engine	120 bhp at 1800 rpm
Suspension	Leaf
Brakes	Triple servo automatic brake adjusters
Turning circle	65′ 8″ (Swept 72′ 11″)
Steering	Marles cam-and-roller

Body details

Overall width	7′ 6″	*Unladen weight*	6 tons 19 cwt.
Seating	35	*Laden weight*	9 tons 3 cwt.

Vehicles built

Leyland Olympic: Met-Cammell

(Top Left) The forerunner of the RF: an A.E.C. prototype underfloor-engined single-decker.

(Bottom Left) One of the contenders for replacement of pre-war Green Line coaches—the Leyland Olympic single-decker.

43 RF Type 1951

WITH THE SUCCESSFUL OPERATION of the A.E.C. prototype UMP 227 an order was placed with A.E.C. for 700 Regal Mark IV with a body mounted by M.C.W. This order represented a return to the semi-integral vehicle with the body mounted on a series of outriggers along the chassis length and not readily detachable from the chassis.

The first order was for 25 private hire vehicles to replace the elderly LTC type some of which had been fitted with oil engines. The colour scheme for these RFs was somewhat unusual; the body was basically green with red window surrounds and a grey roof. To allow universal operation they were restricted to 27′ 6″ overall length.

Then followed the Green Line replacements, allowing the 10T10 vehicles to be diverted to country and central bus work. In this case the overall length went to 30′ which was to continue for the rest of the contract. After the completion of the Green Line series, sufficient central area buses were built to replace all earlier single-deck bus vehicles. Finally the country area received its quota for bus operation. A series of conversions took place in 1956 when RF289–294 were repainted green and fitted with doors and luggage racks for Green Line work. RF295–313 remained red but were renumbered RF514–532, whilst the originals of this batch became RF295 to 313, and were converted for Green Line operation. To complete the central area fleet, RF533–538 were repainted red, and had their doors removed. RF16–25 were transferred to Green Line from Private Hire. Subsequently most RF type buses and coaches were converted to O.M.O. working.

All the vehicles were built as 7′ 6″ wide but mention should be made of 65 vehicles purchased on behalf of B.E.A. to operate the special service from Gloucester Road to London Airport. These had a 1½-decker body, Chiswick-designed but Park Royal-built.

For luxury private hire 15 vehicles were purchased with an 8′ wide body by Eastern Coachworks as supplied to the Tilling organizations. It was classed RFW.

Although the RF gave some initial teething troubles, it has given yeoman service and a few are still running after 22 years. A considerable number of the Green Line RFs were given a restyling including the fitting of twin headlamps on each side.

When delivered all vehicles were fitted with a pilot injection system (Atlas) considerably reducing the diesel knock associated with oil engines. Unfortunately poorer fuel consumption and maintenance problems led to conversion to standard injection.

(*Below*) RF26, allocated to Tunbridge Wells garage, ready for Green Line post-war service.

Chassis details MAKER'S REF: A.E.C. REGAL MK IV—9821 LT

Track	Front 6′ 3½″, rear 5′ 8″ (7′ 6″ vehicle)
Overall length	27′ 6″ and 30′ *Wheelbase* 16′ 4″ (30′ version)
Frame	Channel section with outriggers
Front axle	Reversed Elliot taper roller bearings. Taper roller bearings
Rear axle	Worm gear 4·4/7:1 fully floating parallel bearings
Gearbox	A.E.C. pre-selective epicyclic air pressure 4 speed
Clutch	Fluid flywheel
Engine	A.E.C. 6 cylinder oil A219 9·6 litre underfloor 120 mm. bore 142 mm. stroke 155 bhp at 1800 rpm
Suspension	High deflection leaf Torsion stabiliser rears Shock absorber fronts
Brakes	Air pressure *Steering* A.E.C. worm-and-nut
Turning circle	61′ 0‴

Body details

Overall height	10′ 4½″	*Overall width* 7′ 5½″	
Seating	27′ 6″: 35 30′ 0″: 39, 40 or 41		
Unladen weight	RF1–25: 7 tons 12 cwt.	RF26 7 tons 17 cwt.	RFW: 8 tons 8 cwt.
Laden weight	RF1–25: 9 tons	RF26: 10 tons 8 cwt.	RFW: 10 tons 19 cwt.

Vehicles built

RF   1– 25 27′ 6″ length Private Hire coach 35 seat M.C.W. body
     26–288 30′ 0″ length Greenline coach 39 seat M.C.W. body
    289–513 30′ 0″ length Central bus 41 seat M.C.W. body
    514–700 30′ 0″ length Country bus 41 seat M.C.W. body
    Numbers Subsequently changed (see page 124).
RFW 1–15 30′ × 8′ body Private Hire coach with E.C.W. body 39 seats A.E.C. type 9821E)
BEA   30′ × 8′ special 1½ deck body A.E.C. 9822E. Known by Reg. No. MLL713–762 and NLP636–650 (65 vehicles)

(Below) Central area RF bus; note the absence of doors and the side route number position.

125

(*Above*) RF coach built for Private Hire work.

(*Below*) The RFW coach—also built for Private Hire work, and a comfortable 8 feet wide.

(*Above*) RF for Country area bus services, with folding doors.

(*Left*) A possible replacement for the 1½-decker inter-station coaches: the A.E.C. Regent Mark V.

(*Below*) A B.E.A. 1½-decker for airport to city service.

44 GS Type 1953

THE LEYLAND CUBS had served the outer area of London Transport very well for some 18 years and their replacement by the CR in 1938 had been stopped by the war. A joint specification was drawn up with Guy Motors for a 26-seater bus based on partly the Vixen and partly the Otter chassis. This resulted in a Perkins 6-cylinder oil-engined vehicle with clash gearbox and normal control steering. An attractive body (executed by Eastern Coachworks) was fitted and the vehicle recorded as the GS.

All vehicles were allocated in country service for the sparse traffic routes on which it was not economical to operate a bigger saloon. However, with more economic use of Green Line vehicles in the early morning, it was possible to dispense with these GS vehicles in many cases and finally in the interest of full standardization, agreement was reached to operate the larger RF, or hand the routes over to private operators.

Three were retained for operation of the daily staff bus service from Reigate to Chiswick and one for Abbey Wood/Chiswick until 1973.

One GS was converted as a mobile dressing station for the L.T. St. John Ambulance Brigade at Reigate garage.

A rugged, robust vehicle the GS type stood up to the rigours of London Transport service and its equal has yet to be found in this passenger vehicle range.

(*Below*) A Guy special—GS83.

Chassis details MAKER'S REF: GUY VIXEN/OTTER NORMAL CONTROL

Track	Front 5' 7⅞", rear 5' 6⅛"
Overall length	25' 0½"
Wheelbase	15' 0"
Frame	Channel section steel pressings
Front axle	Reversed Elliot construction I section. Taper roller bearings
Rear axle	Spiral bevel 5·7:1 fully floating taper roller bearings
Gearbox	4 speed constant mesh 2nd
Clutch	11" diameter single plate
Engine	Perkins P6 oil 4·73 litres 3" bore × 5" stroke 63 bhp at 2200 rpm
Suspension	Semi elliptical leaf springs shock absorbers both axles
Brakes	Lockheed Hydrovac
Steering	Bishop cam-and-roller
Turning circle	56' 8"

Body details

Overall height	9' 5½"		*Unladen weight*	4 tons 1 cwt.
Overall width	7' 5½"		*Laden weight*	5 tons 15 cwt.
Seating	26			

Vehicles built

1–84 Normal control 26 seat—ECW body

(Below) Another Green Line contender: the Bristol LS5G. (*see page 130*)

45 Experimental lightweight vehicles

ALTHOUGH the RF programme had recently been completed, thoughts were turning in 1953 to the use of lightweight construction. With the price of fuel, any savings in weight could make a big difference to the fuel bill. Three vehicles were obtained, one each from the principal manufacturers:

Bristol LS5G with Eastern Coachwork body
Leyland Tiger Cub with Saunders Roe body
A.E.C. Chassisless Monocoach with PRV body

All were allocated to Reigate Garage for extensive tests on Route 447 and 711. At the end of the test no decision was made and the vehicles were returned to their owners.

(*Right*) Leyland PSUC 1/1 at Woldingham on Route 447.
          W. J. Haynes

(*Below*) The A.E.C. Monocoach.

Chassis details MAKER'S REF: BRISTOL LS5G

Track	Front 6' 10½", rear 6' 0½"	*Overall length*	30'
Wheelbase	17' 2"		
Frame	$\frac{5}{32}$" steel channel with 8 crossmembers		
Front axle	I section beam taper roller bearings		
Rear axle	Fully floating spiral bevel 5·43:1		
Gearbox	5 speed synchromesh (2, 3, & 4) 5th speed overdrive		
Clutch	16¼" diameter single dry plate		
Engine	Gardner 5 HLW 5 cylinder oil 7·0 litres 107·95 mm. bore × 152·4 mm. stroke 94 bhp at 1700 rpm		
Suspension	Semi-elliptic leaf springs with metalastik shackles shock absorbers on front axle		
Brakes	Clayton Dewandre triple servo manual adjustment		
Turning circle	Swept 65' 8". Turning 59' 2½"	*Steering*	Marles cam-and-roller 20·6:1

Body details

Overall height	10' 2½"	*Unladen weight*	6 tons 7 cwt.
Overall width	8'	*Laden weight*	9 tons 4 cwt.
Seating	45		

Chassis details MAKER'S REF: VEHICLE TYPE TIGER CUB LEYLAND PSUC 1/1

Overall length	30'	*Wheelbase*	16' 2"
Frame	Channel section		
Front axle	I section taper roller bearings thrust buttons for load carrying		
Rear axle	Eaton 2-speed spiral bevel 5·62:1 and 7·81:1 (Note 7·81 locked out for tests)		
Gearbox	4 speed RV 16 direct air operated box		
Clutch	Centrifugal		
Engine	Leyland O350 6 cylinder oil 5·76 litres, pneumatically governed speed 90 bhp at 2200 rpm 240 lbs ft. at 1300 rpm		
Suspension	Semi-elliptical leaf springs with shock absorbers on front axle		
Brakes	Air pressure cam brakes double-ratchet handbrake		
Steering	Marles cam-and-double roller 28·5:1		

Body details

Overall width	8'	*Unladen weight*	5 tons 12 cwt.
Seating	44	*Laden weight*	8 tons 17 cwt.

Chassis details MAKER'S REF: VEHICLE TYPE A.E.C. MONOCOACH

Overall length	30'	*Wheelbase*	16' 4"
Frame	9" deep channel section		
Front axle	I section beam thrust buttons taper roller bearings		
Rear axle	Spiral bevel 5·2/9:1 fully floating		
Gearbox	A.E.C. D 150 (RT) pre-selective gearbox		
Clutch	A.E.C. centrifugal clutch		
Engine	A.E.C. AH 410 6 cylinder oil 6·75 litres 285 lbs fr at 1200 rpm governed 1700 rpm		
Suspension	Leaf springs, shock absorbers front only		
Brakes	Girling with manual adjusters	*Steering*	A.E.C. worm-and-nut 32:1

Body details

Overall width	8'	*Unladen weight*	5 tons 11 cwt.
Seating	44	*Laden weight*	8 tons 8 cwt.

46 **RM Type** 1959

THE ADVENT of the Routemaster vehicle was probably the greatest step forward in bus design not only in London Transport's history but for the bus world in general. The RT and RTL vehicles had replaced the trams, and the trolleybus system was due for replacement from 1959.

Extensive operational research had shown that a 56 passenger vehicle was not the ideal size of vehicle for London, it later being considered that 64 seats was preferable. As the speed of London's traffic is governed, to a large extent, by the speed of the bus, the acceleration requirement was increased accordingly. Better acceleration demanded more consistent braking although not equivalent to that of a private car, for fear of injury to passengers. Although a high standard of comfort was required together with passenger appeal, the need for a speedy, reliable, frequent service was essential.

London Transport, then, set about designing such a vehicle. Firstly the hydraulic braking system had been fully developed under experimental control at Turnham Green and Hounslow on RT type vehicles, starting as far back as 1948. In addition a direct selection transmission was developed on four RT buses, again at Turnham Green. To give an acceptable level of comfort over the current leaf springs, an independent suspension system was developed and fitted to a scrap STL chassis but this was never put to service.

On the body side, a stress skin construction was applied whereby the body carried some of the stresses normally contained within the chassis. As a result of this a 64-seat bus was

(*Left*) SLT56, the prototype Routemaster coded RM1.

(*Right*) Production mechanical components were fitted with a lorry body for test running.

evolved, with only two sub-frames instead of a chassis, weighing in all the same as the 56 seater RT.

It was decided to build four prototype vehicles, two with a PRV body with A.E.C. running units and two by Leyland with their units underneath. In the case of Leyland, one had a Weymann body whereas the other had a coach body by Eastern Coachworks Ltd.

The Commercial Motor Show of 1956 saw RM in all its glory. It gave a pleasing appearance in general, well proportioned curves to the body but unfortunately with a bonnet arrangement that was not in keeping with the general design. The next two, RM 2 and 4, appeared the following year and RM3 arrived in early 1958.

Whilst RM1 was running in service from Cricklewood on Route 2, RM2 was being used for trials to determine whether a smaller engine such as the 7·7 litre as opposed to the 9·6 litre fitted would be a better economical proposition. These trials only confirmed the L.T. belief that a bigger engine derated is far better than a smaller engine uprated.

Finally RM2 was built as an improved version of RM1 with the 9·6 litre engine and allocated to Reigate for operation on 406. This was short lived; it was withdrawn and painted red and allocated to Turnhan Green for Route 91 operation for its working life. RM3 was allocated to Willesden for Route 8 and CRL4 (as it was then known) ran on a number of Green Line routes. This service testing was found to be of great value and many problems that would have arisen in production were cleared well beforehand.

Components began to flow in the first half of 1959 and two buses were fitted as lorries with a sandbag load and driven under simulated service conditions. When the completed vehicles were received in June 1959, some were put to service at selected garages for additional running.

The full entry to service of the RM was on 11 November 1959, when withdrawal of the

trolleybuses started at Poplar and West Ham. Fifty of the vehicles allocated to Poplar were fitted with air suspension at the rear as an alternative to the coil springs, in case the latter left something to be desired. Gradually the RM fleet increased until Fulwell, the last Trolleybus garage was converted on 8 May 1962.

In late 1961 questions were raised as to whether the RM was big enough and LT soon showed that by inserting an extra section in the body a 72-seater could be produced without change to mechanical components. Twenty-four such vehicles were produced and operated from Finchley as a trial. In the meantime production reverted to the 64 seater until RM1253.

At this time there was much talk of one-man-operation of buses (mainly single-deckers, of course) so L.T. were quick to show how easy it was to redesign the Routemaster to a one-man-operated bus and yet retain the engine at the front. This was done by fitting a door immediately behind the near side front wheel and deleting the rear platform. Although unacceptable as such to L.T. (as the driver had to turn round to serve the customer) the principle was adopted with Brighton Corporation on its Leyland PD2 & PD3. Although this bus, RMF1254, never ran in service in London, it visited Manchester, Liverpool and East Kent and was finally sold to Northern General who had by this time purchased a fleet of RMF with long bodies. The only satisfactory way was to use a rear-engined vehicle; an idea not popular with London Transport.

(*Below*) RM2, in its original green livery.

Production continued again with standard RMs until 1452 when a Green Line version of the RM (called RMC) was produced. Other than more comfortable seats, different external livery, power doors at the platform and twin headlamps there was little difference. After these 68, production again reverted to RM until 2217 when it was decided to replace the Green Line RTs on the Aldgate services by a lengthened RMC to be known as RCL. This seemed to set the scene for the remainder of the RM production which was of the lengthened variety with the inserted bay, reverting to RML from 2261.

In 1966 B.E.A. took delivery of 65 RMF type vehicles with the 27′ 6″ bodies for operation on the Airport service from Gloucester Road, the passenger luggage being placed in a two-wheeled trailer towed by the bus.

With the decision of the Bus Reshaping Plan to go 'one-man single-deck', the RM production programme was cut in the prime of life after building 2760 buses After 15 years of operation they are still giving highly satisfactory service and reliability, in this way confirming the foresight of their creator.

During 1976 some of the B.E.A. RM vehicles became surplus to need, and these were purchased by LT to ease the bus shortage of that time. They were operated from Romford North St. garage. Ultimately it is the intention to convert these vehicles for learner duties, freeing conventional RM buses for normal service operation.

For the Queen's Jubilee Celebrations of 1977, 25 RMs were painted silver and ran on central London area routes.

(*Below*) One of the 24 'lengthened' Routemasters—RML 903.

Chassis details MAKER'S REF: A.E.C. R2RH

Track	Front 6′ 8″, rear 6′ 2″
Overall length	27′ 6 $\frac{9}{16}$ ″ (RM & RMC) 29′ 10 $\frac{9}{16}$ ″ (RML & RCL)
Wheelbase	16′ 10″ (RM & RMC) 19′ 2″ (RML & RCL)
Frame	A & B Sub channel section
Front axle	Box—unequal wishbones
Rear axle	Spiral bevel 5·22:1 (buses) 4·7 (coaches) taper roller bearings fully floating
Gearbox	A.E.C. direct selection/automatic 4 speed electrical control, air-pressure-operated
Clutch	Fluid flywheel
Engine	A.E.C. AV 590 Leyland 0600 A.E.C. AV 690 (mainly RCL) 9·6 litre 9·8 litre 115 bhp at 1800 rpm 120 mm. × 142 mm. 11·3 litre 150 bhp at 1800 rpm 130 mm. × 142 mm.
Suspension	Coil spring front and rear (Coaches—air suspension rear)
Brakes	Continuous flow split hydraulic power
Steering	A.E.C. worm-and-nut, power-assisted
Turning circle	60′ 0″ ⎱RM 67′ 0″ ⎱RML 60′ 0″ ⎱RM
	62′ 0″ (swept) ⎰RMC 69′ 0″ ⎰RCL 62′ 0″ (swept) ⎰RML

Body details

Overall height 14′ 4 $\frac{7}{16}$ ″   *Overall width* 7′ 11 $\frac{5}{8}$ ″

RM

Seating inside 28   *Seating outside* 36
Unladen weight 7 tons 7 cwt.   *Laden weight* 11 tons 10 cwt.

RMC

Seating inside 25   *Seating outside* 32
Unladen weight 7 tons 16 cwt.   *Laden weight* 11 tons 10 cwt.

RML

Seating inside 32   *Seating outside* 40
Unladen weight 7 tons 14 cwt.   *Laden weight* 12 tons 6 cwt.

RCL

Seating inside 29   *Seating outside* 36
Unladen weight 8 tons 3 cwt.   *Laden weight* 12 tons 7 cwt.

Vehicles built

RM1 & 2	Prototype A.E.C. bus	P.R.V. body
RM3	Prototype Leyland bus (originally RML3)	Weymann body
CRL4	Prototype Leyland coach (now RMC4)	Eastern Coachworks body
RM5–879	Production RM	P.R.V. body
RML880–903	Experimental batch 30′ 72 seater	P.R.V. body
RM904–1253	Production	P.R.V. body
RMF1254	Experimental forward entrance RM 30′ 69 passengers	P.R.V. body
RM1255–1452	Production RM	P.R.V. body
RMC1453–1520	Green Line coach fitted with doors	P.R.V. body
RM1521–2217	Production RM	P.R.V. body
RCL2218–2260	30′ coach with doors	P.R.V. body
RML2261–2760	Production 30′ bus (Central and Country)	P.R.V. body
BEA601–665	27′ 6″ version of RMF operated for B.E.A.	P.R.V. body

(*Above*) Prototype Green Line RM double-decker—CRL4. The side advertisement proclaims the Routemaster coach to be London Transport's coach of the future.

(*Below*) Another prototype—the forward entrance RMF1254.

(*Above*) The production version of the RM bus—RM73.

(*Top Right*) The lengthened coach as finally placed into service: RCL2219.

(*Bottom Right*) Routemaster for B.E.A. services —this version based on the ideas involved with the RMF bus. The trailer is, of course, for luggage reception.

(*Below*) The production version of the Routemaster coach—RMC1463.

(Above) Former B.E.A. RM, at Chiswick Works, awaiting return to bus duties.

(Left) RM442 specially painted as an example for the 25RMs used to mark London Transport's contribution to the Queen's Silver Jubilee celebrations in 1977.

(Below) RM1368, after conversion to a single-decker, following arson attack.

47 **RW Type** 1960

In 1960 London Transport purchased 3 underfloor engine vehicles with the engine, fluid flywheel and gearbox as a combined unit amidship of the chassis. They were fitted with a Willowbrook body with separate entrance and exits for one-man-operation in the country area. The 3 vehicles moved as a group around country garages but were not popular either from an operating or engineering standpoint. The drivers, in particular, found it difficult to draw up at the stops in the country lanes to allow passengers to get on or off the vehicle freely. Once again London Transport's unsatisfactory experience of power packs in a chassis was highlighted, giving rise to continual flywheel trouble.

After their unsuccessful experience these vehicles were sold out of service.

Chassis details MAKER'S REF: A.E.C. 2MU2RA

Track	Front 6' 6⅞", rear 5' 11"	*Overall length*	30'
Wheelbase	16' 4"	*Frame*	Channel
Front axle	Reversed Elliot taper roller bearings		
Rear axle	Fully floating 4·7 5·22:1		
Gearbox	Planetary direct selection air-operated		
Clutch	Fluid flywheel	*Engine*	A.E.C. AH 470 6 cylinder oil
Suspension	Leaf springs shock absorbers on front		
Brakes	Air pressure	*Steering*	A.E.C. worm-and-nut

Body details

Overall width 8' 0"	*Seating*	42

Unladen weight 6 tons 1 cwt.
RW1–3 had entrance and exit doors and bodies by Willowbrook

(*Below*) A.E.C. Reliance bus RW3.

142

48 TT Type 1963

Special vehicles were commisioned by the Dartford Tunnel Authority to carry cycles through the Dartford Tunnel between the hours of 06 00 and 22 00, as regulations prevented cyclists from using the tunnel in the normal way during these times. Outside these hours nocturnal cyclists could pass under pedal power. These were Ford Thames commercial chassis with special cycle carrying accommodation.

The 'TT' type vehicles were designed by L.T. to carry both the cyclists and their cycles through the tunnel. Loading was achieved from special platforms at each end of the tunnel, the passengers travelling upstairs. Operation commenced on 18 November 1963 with a service of four buses (and an engineering spare), all being supplied from Dartford garage.

The anticipated traffic did not arrive and after a short while the service as such was reduced to one vehicle which was finally withdrawn on 31 October 1965. From this date Land Rovers were used by the Tunnel Authority.

Chassis details MAKER'S REF: FORD THAMES TRADER (PSV)

Track	5' 10"	*Overall length*	30'
Wheelbase	17' 8½"	*Frame*	Normal channel
Rear axle	Fully floating Hypoid 6·167:1	*Gearbox*	Synchromesh 4 speed
Clutch	Semi-centrifugal single dry plate		
Engine	Ford 6D diesel 5416 cc 100 bhp at 2500 rpm 242 lbs ft torque at 1500 rpm		
Suspension	Heavy duty leaf springs	*Brakes*	Hydraulic servo
Turning circle	66' 0"	*Steering*	24·7:1 ratio

Body details

Overall height 14' 3⅛"		*Overall width* 7' 10"	
Seating 30		*Carrying capacity* 30 cycles	
Unladen weight 6 tons		*Laden weight* 8·5 tons	
Angle of tilt 28° TT. 1-5 (Strachans body)			

(*Left*) Dartford Tunnel cycle-carrying bus.

143

49 RX Type 1962

A.E.C. revived the name of Renown (previously the 'LT' type) for a lowbridge vehicle with conventional seating instead of employing a sunken gangway upstairs. The transmission line was off-set with the gearbox situated under the staircase, allowing a fairly low saloon floor. Because the engine was situated at its normal height the driver's visibility was severely restricted. One vehicle was operated on hire, coded RXI (PRV body) and ran from Northfleet Country Bus garage. It did not find favour either with L.T. or other operators and the model 'died'.

Chassis details MAKER'S REF: 3B2RA AEC RENOWN

Overall length	30'
Wheelbase	18' 3½"
Frame	Bolted cross section channel
Front axle	Forged I section beam taper roller bearings
Rear axle	Off set double reduction spiral bevel
Gearbox	Monocontrol direct air selection 4 speed
Clutch	Fluid flywheel
Engine	A.E.C. AV 590 6 cylinder oil 120 mm. bore $\times$ 142 mm. stroke 140 bhp at 1800 rpm
Suspension	Leaf springs front air suspension rear
Brakes	Air pressure
Turning circle	66'
Steering	A.E.C. worm-and-nut

Body details

Overall width 8' 0"

(*Left*) A.E.C. Renown double-decker, on hire to London Transport.

50 XF Type 1965

THE POPULARITY of the conventional double-decker with open rear platform was declining in 1965 apart from London. As a means of checking whether the front entrance, rear engine double-decker offered any hidden advantages of which London Transport were not aware, it was decided to purchase eight Daimler Fleetlines for Country service and fifty Atlanteans for Central service. This gave the added advantage of making a comparison between the Fleetline and Atlantean on a mechanical basis.

The eight vehicles were allocated to East Grinstead for operation on Route 424. It was here that the experiment was tried whereby the upper deck was closed off during off-peak periods and the bus became a one-man-operated vehicle, while at other times a conductor was carried.

Although the Fleetline had been in production for several years, London conditions of operation showed a few shortcomings which were improved and overcome. In view of the better running of the Fleetline compared with the Atlantean, an exchange of

(*Below*) XF2 after delivery at Chiswick.

vehicles was made between East Grinstead and Highgate for Route 271, so that the Fleetlines had the opportunity of running under Central London conditions.

After the return of these vehicles to their own garage, the 'Blue Arrow' service was opened up in Stevenage (SV) in December 1969 for which 3 Fleetline were used, namely XF6, 7 and 8. For a few days these vehicles ran in their blue livery but, on 1 January 1970, the legal name was changed to London Country Bus Services Ltd. To cover for the missing three Fleetlines, three Atlanteans were drafted to East Grinstead, ultimately being painted green.

XF3 was fitted with a Cummins V8 engine which meant extensive alterations at the rear end but after a number of engine failures it was decided to be uneconomic to maintain it. Although it has been long since out of service, it is understood as this book is published that it will be shortly returned to service fitted with a Gardner engine. The purpose of this particular experiment was to try and find an alternative to the limited quantities of Gardner engines which, at that time, controlled the supply of Fleetline vehicles.

Although part of the L.C.B.S. story, the introduction of the Metropolitan Scanias for the 'Superbus' service at Stevenage enabled the three Blue Arrows to be withdrawn and returned to East Grinstead.

Chassis details MAKER'S REF: DAIMLER FLEETLINE

Track	Front 6' 7½", rear 6' 0"		
Overall length	30' 6"	*Wheelbase*	16' 3"
Frame	Channel section alloy steel pressings		
Front axle	'H' section steel stamping taper roller bearings		
Rear axle	Two stage reduction spiral bevel spur gear. Drop down axle. Taper roller bearings		
Gearbox	'Diamatic' air-operated epicyclic 4 speed transfer box		
Clutch	Fluid flywheel		
Engine	Gardner 6 cylinder oil 6LX 10·45 litre		
Brakes	Split system air pressure diaphragm-operated		
Suspension	Leaf spring with shock absorbers		
Steering	Worm-and-nut, power-assisted		
Turning circle	61' 6"	69' (swept)	

Body details

Overall height	14' 4¹³⁄₁₆"	*Unladen weight*	9 tons 1 cwt.
Overall width	8' 0"	*Laden weight*	13 tons 14 cwt.
Seating	inside 31, outside 41		
Angle of tilt	28°		

Note: XF 3 has been fitted with a Cummins V6 engine

Vehicles built

XF 1–8 Standard P.R.V. body—all now L.C.B.S.
6, 7 & 8 were painted blue for operation on Blue Arrow Service, Stevenage. Taken over by L.C.B.S. January 1970. Restored to conventional service July 1972.

(*Top Right*) The Blue Arrow concept—a scheme involving pre-booked works services for the Country Bus area began late 1969. The experiment was confined to Stevenage garage, and this Fleetline was photographed whilst still in London Transport ownership, although bearing the new London Country name.

(*Bottom Right*) Atlantean XA bus which ran on central London routes. (*see page 148*).

147

51 **XA Type** (Atlantean) 1965

AS MENTIONED in the previous chapter, the purchase of these vehicles formed part of a service experiment to test the capabilities of a front entrance, rear-engined double-deck bus in all conditions.

As the Leyland Atlantean was more readily available than the Fleetline a greater proportion of Atlantean were purchased. Although fitted with similar PRV bodies as the Fleetline, the Leyland chassis was only fitted with single line braking, compared to the split system on the Daimler vehicle. Brake adjustment was a manual task.

The Atlantean was put to work on Route 24 out of Chalk Farm and 271 from Highgate giving rise to serious service problems. After a time an exchange was made between Chalk Farm and Tottenham garages on one hand and Highgate and Stamford Hill garages on the other hand, to replace RMLs on Routes 76 and 67, and a strict observation was kept of their performance so that an accurate assessment could be made between the two distinct types of vehicles. Reference has already been made in the previous chapter to the temporary exchange made with the Fleetline at East Grinstead.

Because of the Blue Arrow experiment at Stevenage, XA47, 48 and 49 were transferred to East Grinstead where they remained, painted green, and never returned to the L.T. fleet.

By the time the first vehicle overhaul arrived, one-man-operation of double-deckers had been agreed and the vehicles were out-shopped as O.M.O. for service on the 'C' express routes at Croydon with the exception of a few for Route 234 which was a conventional O.M.O. service. It was probably here that the Atlanteans performed at their best and appeared to be more suited to this type of operation instead of heavy city work.

An opportunity presented itself to sell these 47 vehicles to Hong Kong in 1973, and L.C.B.S. contributed the other 3.

In fairness to Leyland, the current Atlantean known as the AN68 incorporates many improvements over that tested by L.T., such as the charged coupling, split braking, automatic brake adjustment, which overcame much of London Transport's criticism.

Chassis details MAKER'S REF: LEYLAND PDR1/1

Track	Front 6' 5¼", rear 5' 11½"	*Overall length*	30'
Wheelbase	16' 3"	*Frame*	Channel section alloy steel
Front axle	I section taper roller		
Rear axle	Fully floating spiral bevel 3·083:1 ratio angle drive 1·263:1		
Gearbox	Direct acting 4 speed epicyclic fully automatic		
Clutch	Fluid flywheel with lock-up clutch		
Engine	Leyland 0680 6 cylinder		
Brakes	Single line air pressure diaphragm operated		
Suspension	Leaf springs with shock absorbers		
Steering	Marles cam-and-roller, power-assisted		
Turning circle	61' 3" 71' 0" (swept)		

Body details

Overall height	14' 4 11⁄16"	*Unladen weight*	8 tons 18 cwt.
Overall width	8' 0"	*Laden weight*	13 tons 10 cwt.
Seating inside	31	*Seating outside*	41

Vehicles built

XA1–50 Standard P.R.V. body
47, 48 and 49 were transferred to Country Area, subsequently L.C.B.S., then to Hong Kong

52 **RC Type** 1965

TO IMPROVE the Green Line image, 14 coaches of the latest A.E.C. Reliance were purchased, employing a Willowbrook body. The seating was of a luxurious pattern with head rests and panoramic windows. To enhance further the standard of comfort, air suspension was employed for all axles. In order to accommodate 49 passengers in this luxury, the vehicle was 36′ 0″ long, being the first of this length to be operated in London by London Transport. A 5-speed gearbox was fitted, (direct air, Wilson type) to give a higher top speed and yet maintain good startability required on Green Line operation.

The vehicles were allocated to Windsor (WR) and Dunton Green (DG) for the 705 service and it was not long before service problems arose. Since little experience had ever been gained with air suspension on front axles, it was not surprising that shudder and vibration occurred because of inadequate location of the axle. Because of this, and the absence of automatic brake adjusters, they were not very popular with operating crews.

A scheme was evolved with A.E.C. to rework the brakes by employing the 'S' cam idea, instead of the sliding shoe. This was done by carrying out axle changes and at the same time the coaches were repainted from the white with a green band to the conventional Green Line green and lighter band.

Since their introduction in 1965 these vehicles have been run on a variety of routes including short spells on 725, 727 and were based on Grays (GY), L.C.B.S.

One vehicle (RC11) has been written off, after a fire arising from an engine failure.

(*Below*) A.E.C. Reliance RC coach, as originally delivered.

Chassis details MAKER'S REF: A.E.C. 4U2RA

Track	Front 6′ 8⅝″, rear 5′ 11⅛″	*Overall length*	35′ 4¾″
Wheelbase	18′ 7″	*Frame*	Channel section
Front axle	Reversed Elliot taper roller bearings		
Rear axle	Spiral bevel 4·08 ratio, taper roller bearings		
Gearbox	5 speed direct selection epicyclic		
Clutch	Fluid flywheel		
Engine	A.E.C. AH 691 6 cylinder oil 130 mm. bore × 142 mm. stroke		
Brakes	Split air pressure diaphragm-operated		
Suspension	Air suspension both axles	*Turning circle*	62′ 0″ 71′ 0″ (swept)
Steering	Worm-and-nut, power-assisted		

Body details

Overall height	10′ 0¾″	*Unladen weight*	8 tons 10 cwt.
Overall width	8′ 2½″	*Laden weight*	11 tons 14 cwt.
Seating	49	*Angle of tilt*	35°

Vehicles built   RC 1–14 Willowbrook body, now with L.C.B.S.

53 EC Type 1966

TO LAUNCH its Executive Express service (for businessmen to be driven direct from the air terminal to the aeroplane), B.E.A. purchased eight A.E.C. Reliances to an alternative arrangement to that of the RC coaches. These Reliances employed a ZF spur gearbox with synchromesh on certain speeds and having 6 speeds in all. Suspension was by leaf springs. Although the body was similar to the RC it was built by Duple (who own Willowbrook). The vehicles were passed to LT for operation beside the other 65RM.

As 'Executive Express' has now been withdrawn, these vehicles are no longer in service and some have been transferred to Scottish airports for passenger carrying duties.

Chassis details MAKER'S REF: A.E.C. RELIANCE 2U3RA

Track	Front 6′ 8⅝″, rear 5′ 11⅞″		
Overall length	35′ 4¾″	*Wheelbase*	18′ 7″
Frame	Channel section dropped tail extension		
Front axle	Reversed Elliot taper roller bearings		
Rear axle	Spiral bevel 4·08:1 fully floating opposed taper roller bearings		
Gearbox	Synchro/constant mesh (ZF type) 6 speed		
Clutch	Single plate hydraulically operated		
Engine	A.E.C. AH 590 6 cylinder oil 120 mm. bore × 142 mm. stroke 145 bhp at 1800 rpm		
Suspension	Leaf springs with telescopic dampers		
Brakes	Air-pressure-operated, drum brakes		
Turning circle	62′ 0″		
Steering	A.E.C. worm-and-nut, power-assisted		

Body details

Overall width	8′ 0″	*Seating*	49

Vehicles built   8

150

(*Above*) A.E.C. Reliance coach, with ZF
gearbox seen here at Heathrow Airport on
B.E.A. service.

(*Below*) The rear-engined Routemaster FRM1.

54 FRM Type 1967

IT BECAME fairly obvious after the 1964 Phelps Brown committee of enquiry into the pay and conditions of London Bus crews that one-man operation of double-deckers would be authorized. L.T. had already produced a version of the Routemaster (RMF) that could be operated as 'one-man', but was not thought to be acceptable in London. Therefore, it set to work to produce a one-man double-decker which would be acceptable by all concerned and utilise as much of the Routemaster principles as possible. At that time it was felt that the only suitable place for the engine to suit one-man-operation was at the rear transverse. Due thought and consideration was given to the design of installations so that each component could be removed from under the bonnet without the need for removing the engine. The hydraulic braking and power steering was taken from the successful RM design and the body used about 60 per cent of the components of the RM.

Plans were made to build five vehicles one for L.T. service, one for A.E.C. experimental and the remainder as demonstrators by A.E.C., Park Royal and others. In the event only one vehicle was ever finished, which L.T. put into service in conjunction with the XA on Route 76 from Tottenham (AR). It was perhaps unfortunate that the vehicle was fitted with an air conditioning scheme which would eliminate the need for drop windows. This system worked admirably under stable conditions but it was not sensitive enough to change and eventually drop windows had to be re-instated.

When the XA moved to Croydon, FRM1 was also transferred there to operate on Route 234. When this passed to Fleetline operation the FRM1 was allocated to Potters Bar on one-bus Route 284, and was much sought after by amateur cameramen. As this book goes to press, it is being renovated for the Round London Sightseeing Tour.

Bus design by L.T., in conjunction with A.E.C., had reached its peak but the book was to be closed, for a new era was to start with the single-deck bus. Another 10 years were to elapse before new designs were put in hand for London.

Chassis details MAKER'S REF: EXPERIMENTAL FRONT ENTRANCE RM

Track	Front 6′ 9″, rear 6′ 3″		
Overall length	31′ 5″	*Wheelbase*	16′ 10″
Frame	Rear B sub frames channel section		
Front axle	Unequal wishbones fitted to body structure		
Rear axle	Spiral bevel 5·22:1 ratio taper-roller bearings fully floating		
Gearbox	S.C.G. air operated direct selection/automatic/4 speed electrical control air pressure operated—combined transfer box		
Clutch	Fluid flywheel 18″ diameter		
Engine	A.E.C. AV 691 11·3 litre 6 cylinder oil. 130 mm. bore × 142 mm. stroke 150 bhp at 1800 rpm		
Suspension	Coil spring front (independent) air suspension rear (rigid axle)		
Brakes	Continuous flow split-hydraulic lockheed power		
Steering	A.E.C. worm-and-nut, power-assisted		
Turning circle	57′ 6″ 68′ 2″ (swept)		

Body details

Overall height	14′ 5 $\frac{1}{16}$″	*Unladen weight*	8 tons 9 cwt.
Overall width	8′ 0″	*Laden weight*	13 tons 6 cwt.
Seating inside	31	*Seating outside*	41

55 MB Type 1968

AS PART OF the experiment to carry large numbers of passengers over short distances with large capacity single-deck vehicles, L.T. ordered six A.E.C. Merlin with Strachan bodies carrying 25 seated and 50 standing passengers coded XMS. These entered service on a new Route 500 between Victoria and Marble Arch, with only one stop on route (at Hyde Park Corner), as from April 1966.

Nine similar buses were built with similar separate entrance and exit doors for the country area but only XMB15 remained green. The other eight were ultimately repainted red for working on Route 500 on a rotational basis. Although this route carried a large number of passengers at a fixed fare, the conditions were not as arduous as normal London bus work, and it only operated Mondays–Fridays. The vehicles gave little trouble, apart from changes that had to be made to braking ratios between the axles to overcome tendency to wheel-locking during wet weather.

Because of the popularity of the 500 service, it was decided to open up some more routes between main line London stations, calling the whole group of routes 'Red Arrow' services. In consequence the buses were coded MBA. At the same time the Bus Reshaping Plan 1966 announced that there was to be a change from double-deck to single-deck, with shortened routes and at a flat fare. These were to be known as satellite routes and operated by similar vehicles, without the change-giving facility on the Red Arrows. They were coded MBS. Included in this first big order for Merlins, were 33 MB for the Country area, fully seated but with separate entrance and exit doors, mainly for use in the Reigate and Watford areas with standard fare collection method. 52 were ordered for outer Central area with only front entrance/exit and coded MB. These vehicles had one big difference in the chassis, in that A.E.C. fitted its own foundation brake equipment at London Transport's insistence because of service troubles experienced on the RC vehicles (which had the same equipment as the XMS and XMB). The body-builder for all this order was M.C.W. In all other respects these vehicles were to a manufacturer's standard specification.

(*Below*) The Red Arrow MBA bus.

Criticisms were received from the drivers that the driving position on these vehicles was poor in that insufficient view was given of the road and the relationship between driver and passenger was at a disadvantage to the driver. L.T., therefore, arranged for A.E.C. to bring the driving position higher by building a false floor on the chassis at the cab position. This, in fact, gave the same relationship between driver, seat, pedals and road as the RM (which has been recognized as one of the national standards for the Bus Grant Scheme).

The introduction of this improved standard coincided with a further change in specification. A.E.C. was part of British Leyland and the fruits of rationalization were beginning to take effect. The A.E.C. flywheel and direct-selection gearbox had been dropped to be replaced by a rationalised fluid flywheel and gearbox. A revised power pack mounting arrangement was introduced. Because of these modifications a new chassis code was created (2MB as compared with 1MB for the earlier order). Further orders were placed for Red Arrows (MBA), Country and Central Standee (MBS) and Central fully seated

(*Below*) MBS79, used on 'satellite' suburban bus services. They were inappropriate for heavy duty short haul work in London.

(*Bottom*) Full-seated version of MB bus, designed for one-man-operation, with single door.

(MB) taking the fleet total to 665, including the 15 XMS/B.

With operation of a large number of this 36' long type of vehicle considerable difficulties were experienced in negotiating routes because of obstructions, such as parked vehicles. Congestion was also caused by buses being unable to pull into bus stops to allow other traffic to pass. It became clear that the 36' overall length was too long for all but a few of the routes such as 500 and, therefore, a 33' length was suggested as a better proposition. The 36' length was chosen in the first instance since it was possible to have the same capacity, as the double-decker it was envisaged would be replaced.

Gradually the DMS has replaced the MB wherever possible giving preference to withdrawal of the 1MB first. Surplus MB types were hired to L.C.B.S. to help overcome its vehicle shortage problems. However, there remain in service a number of MBA Red Arrow buses.

The improvements of the Bus Reshaping Plan 1966 have not materialized and a reversion to double-deckers (in some cases, with conductors) is in hand. Added to that is the fact that the Merlin bus has failed to stand up to the rigours of London service, and has presented a very high maintenance cost.

Chassis details MAKER'S REF: A.E.C.—3P2R & 4P2R

Track	Front 6' 9½", rear 5' 11⅝"	*Overall length*	35' 8"
Wheelbase	18' 6"	*Frame*	Channel
Front axle	Reversed Elliot taper roller		
Rear axle	Single reduction spiral bevel 5·22:1 ratio		
Gearbox	3P2R A.E.C. direct-operating epicyclic 4P2R rationalised fully automatic for central area		
Clutch	Fluid flywheel—3P2R—A.E.C. 4P2R rationalised		
Engine	A.E.C. AH691 130 mm. bore 142 mm. stroke 6 cylinder oil 690 cu. ins capacity		
Brakes	Split system air pressure diaphragm operated		
Suspension	Leaf springs with shock absorbers		
Steering	3P2R cam-and-roller, Marles 4P2R cam-and-roller, Adwest both power-assisted		
Turning circle	61' 71' (swept)		

Body details

Overall height	10' 4"	*Overall width* 8' 2½"	
Seating 25	*Fully seated* MB 50/45	*Standard* MBA/S 73*	

* Additional/single seats fitted later reducing the capacity to 66 (MBA).

CENTRAL STANDEE

Unladen weight 8 tons 1 cwt.		*Laden weight* 12 tons 17 cwt.

Vehicles built

1MB types

XMS1–6 ⎫ (as built) XMS1–14 ⎫ total 15 Strachan body
XMB1–9 ⎭   XMB15 (formerly XMB1) ⎭

MBA16–31	Red Arrow bus. M.C.W. body, centre exit
MBS32– 80	Central Standee bus. M.C.W. body, centre exit
MB81–113	Country seated bus. M.C.W. body, centre exit
MB114–165	Central seated bus. M.C.W. body, no centre exit

2MB types

MBA166–193	Red Arrow bus. M.C.W. body, centre exit
MBS194–303*	Country & Central standee bus. M.C.W. body, centre exit
MB304–397	Central seated bus. M.C.W. body, no centre exit
MBS398–615†	Country & Central standee bus. M.C.W. body, centre exit
MB616–665	Central seated bus. M.C.W. body, no centre exit

* 270–303 Country   † 398–438 Country

56 **SM Type** 1970

HAVING ACCEPTED the fact that 33' was to be the new length for a single-decker in London, it was no longer possible to fit the existing Merlin engine without a complete re-design of the transmission on the lines of the Bristol RE. The overhang of a vehicle is limited to a percentage of the wheelbase, precluding the Merlin engine. It was decided, therefore, to fit the AH505 which was considerably shorter and could be installed on the same lines as the MB. To get the equivalent power/torque the engine speed had to be increased from 1800 to 2200 RPM which has meant a change in the rear axle ratio. With the shorter vehicle and smaller engine there was a weight advantage in favour of nearly ½ ton for the SM vehicle (as it was to be called).

For the orders placed three body-builders were involved: Marshall, Park Royal and M.C.W. Apart from the first 50 by Marshall, all have a centre exit body. Included in these orders were two batches totalling 138 on behalf of L.C.B.S. which, although carrying LT bonnet numbers in sequence, have Surrey Council registrations.

Although the Swift has been a more manageable vehicle, the poor engine life has once again proved the old maxim that, for London at least, a bigger engine derated is a better proposition than a small one uprated.

Along with the MB all the SMs are to be withdrawn in favour of Leyland Nationals (see p. 165).

Chassis details MAKER'S REF: A.E.C. 4MP2R

Track	Front 6' 9½", rear 5' 11⅝"	Overall length	32' 10¼"
Wheelbase	16' 6"	Frame	Channel
Front axle	Reversed Elliot taper roller		
Rear axle	Single reduction spiral bevel 4·8 ratio		
Gearbox	Leyland rationalised direct acting epicyclic 4 speed. Fully automatic for central area.		
Clutch	Leyland rationalised fluid flywheel		
Engine	A.E.C. AH505 116 mm. bore 130 mm. stroke 502 cu. ins capacity		
Brakes	Split system air-pressure diaphragm-operated		
Suspension	Leaf springs with shock absorbers		
Steering	Adwest cam-and-roller, power-assisted		
Turning circle	65'		

Body details

Overall height	10' 1"	Overall width	8' 2½"
Fully seated	SM 42	Standee	SMS 67

Note: Country fully-seated 38

CENTRAL STANDEE

Unladen weight	7 tons 12 cwt.	Laden weight	12 tons 0 cwt.

Vehicles built

SM1–50	Central. Marshall body
SMS51–100	Central. P.R.V. body, centre exit
SM101–148	Country. P.R.V. body, centre exit
SMS149–223	Central. Marshall body, centre exit
SMS224–448	Central. P.R.V. body, centre exit
SM449–538	Country. M.C.W. body, centre exit
SMS539–838	Central. M.C.W. body, centre exit

(*Above*) SM47, a Marshall bodied Swift bus.   (*Below*) SMS58 'satellite' standee-type Swift.

57 **Metro Scania** 1973

M.C.W. had entered into an agreement with Scania Vabis to market in Great Britain a complete vehicle with body by M.C.W. and employing running units by Scania of Sweden. The completed vehicle employs two sub frames much on the lines of the RM but is supplied to M.C.W. as a one-piece unit. This is then cut apart and can be used for any wheelbase.

In order to assess the suitability of the Scania for London operation a demonstrator was obtained and given a preliminary test. In general the vehicle was not built to L.T. requirements but it was considered prudent to make one or two modifications before it entered service on Route 99 at Plumstead (AM).

Although a further policy change had brought the double-decker back into favour again, it was nevertheless decided to purchase six single-deck vehicles. This was to enable experience to be gained from the mechanical design which it was known was to be incorporated in a new double deck vehicle—known as the Metropolitan.

See Chapter 60 for specification of the MS itself.

(*Below*) The Scania demonstrator bus, on evaluation trials.

(*Right*) One of the early production DMS buses.

58 **DMS Type** 1971

ONCE AGREEMENT had been reached with the unions on one-man operation of double-deck vehicles, opportunity was taken to end the single-deck programme. This would bring improvements to all concerned—better manoeuvrability in traffic, more garage space, and reduced pit lengths for maintenance.

Based on the experience of the earlier trial of Fleetlines and Atlanteans it was decided to opt for the Fleetline. It fitted in better with L.T. maintenance, in that engine, gearboxes were mounted independently, and that one could be removed without disturbing the other. Although both vehicles were rear-engined, the Fleetline with its Gardner engine did not suffer so much from the overheating problem that seems to arise with most rear engine installations.

In the first instance 17 vehicles were ordered to be fitted with a basic standard P.R.V. body. The chassis incorporated a minimum of variations. Before they could be delivered, it became necessary to order a further 100 in order to ensure continuity of supply as the Fleetline chassis was in great demand. These later 100 included a few alterations introduced by Daimler in their annual updating procedure.

The first 117 Daimlers were allocated initially to Shepherd's Bush, replacing Routemasters on Route 220, and to Brixton on Route 95. One or two service problems arose,

mainly from a world shortage of nickel steel at this time which gave rise to transmission problems. Bearing this point in mind one or two other changes were decided upon which created a re-coding for the next 250 order (still to be with P.R.V. bodies).

A few operators of the Fleetline vehicle had specified the Leyland 0680 engine instead of the Gardner 6LXB mainly on the grounds of initial cost. To give two sources of supply, L.T. decided to fit a Leyland 0680 in DMS132.

For the next order of 1600 vehicles, the body contract was split between P.R.V. (880 bodies) and M.C.W. (720 bodies). Although the bodies were similar externally, each builder utilized its own construction and there was little interchangeability between panels, glasses etc. For the chassis it was decided to fit a large number of Leyland 0680 engines. It was at this time Gardner suffered industrial action which led to a complete stoppage in the supply of engines and the fitment of Leyland engines was increased.

Because of the success of the Jaguar car sales (which was part of the specialist car division of British Leyland, controlling Daimlers) there was the need for expansion at Coventry. This was not possible at Browns Lane where the Jaguar cars were built and it was decided to take over the bus production factory at Coventry (Radford Road). Production of Fleetline was transfered to Leyland's Faringdon Works in 1972 but at the start it was decided not to make any changes in design. In any such move, production does not run without hitches and by the end of 1974 the production of the 1600 vehicles was about 6 months in arrears.

With legislation impending to quieten vehicle noise emission, development work was carried out on DMS88 which ended up with air intakes and outlets for the engine compartment as two chimneys either side of the rear engine-pod. Further work was done in quietening the engine itself and also the fitment of undertrays. Most of this work was concentrated on the Leyland engine as this was slightly noisier. A further vehicle has now been

(*Below*) DMS2366, the B20 with 'quietened' engine unit.

produced to reach the ultimate noise level which will employ a turbo-charged engine to assist, not only with noise levels but in maintaining a smoke free exhaust for a greater time. This is to be known as the quiet Fleetline, (Leyland code reference B20).

The last order on British Leyland for 1976 called for 687 DMS of which many are to be fitted with noise suppression gear to give a reading of 81 dbA. Amongst this order will be vehicles with Gardner engines but it is unlikely they will be to the extreme quiet figure.

In the interest of causing less congestion, it has now been decided to employ conductors in the Central area and some of the vehicles in the 1600 contract have been built with seats in place of the automatic fare equipment. As fully-seated buses they carry 71 seats with provision for standing passengers compared with the 89 when operated as a standee bus. The fully seated buses are lettered as DM.

Throughout the DMS programme there have been one or two changes in external livery. Only 250 were painted with a white band at inter-floor level which gave a relief to the expanse of red. In the interest of cheaper production costing this was deleted later. The entrance doors have now been painted in yellow to emphasise passenger entrance as opposed to exit, which will apply to one man buses. Changes have been made to the L.T. 'roundel' in that it has been made solid and moved from the lower panel position to one above the entrance door. A more recent change has been to pick out the window surrounds for the upper deck in white although this will not apply retrospectively.

Chassis details MAKER'S REF: DAIMLER FLEETLINE

Overall length	30′ 6″	*Wheelbase*	16′ 3″
Frame	Channel section alloy steel pressing reinforced		
Front axle	'H' section steel stamping taper roller bearings		
Rear axle	Two stage reduction drop down spiral bevel—spur gear taper roller bearings transfer box		
Gearbox	Diamatic air-operated epicyclic 4 speed fully automatic		
Clutch	Fluid flywheel		
Engine	Gardner 6 cylinder oil 6 LXB 10·45 litre or Leyland 0680		
Brakes	Split system air pressure diaphragm operated		
Suspension	Heavy duty leaf spring with shock absorber		
Steering	Worm-and-nut	*Turning circle*	69′ (swept)

Body details

Overal height 14′ 6″		*Overall width* 8′ 2½″	
Seating (Standee) outside 44		*Seating (Standee) inside* 24	
Standees 21			
Seating (all seats) outside 44		*Seating (all seats) inside* 27	
Unladen weight 9 tons 7 cwt.		*Laden weight* 15 tons 3 cwt.	

Vehicles built

DMS		
	1– 367	Gardner engine. P.R.V. body
	368–1967	Mixed Gardner and Leyland engines (880 P.R.V. 720 M.C.W.)
	1968–2037	Leyland engine. M.C.W. body
	2038–2057	Gardner engine. M.C.W. body
	2058–2127	Leyland engine. P.R.V. body
	2128–2166	Gardner engine. P.R.V. body
	2167–2246	Gardner engine. M.C.W. body
	2247–2346	Leyland (B20) engine. M.C.W. body
	2347–2646	Leyland (B20) engine. P.R.V. body

The B20 is a specially quietened vehicle, incorporating a turbo-charged Leyland 0680 engine.

59 FS Type 1973

LONDON TRANSPORT were requested by the G.L.C. to operate minibus services in four areas of community relationships at no loss to L.T. The areas concerned were Enfield (serving a hospital), Bromley (serving a railway station), Stockwell (serving Dulwich village) and Highgate. 17 vehicles were involved in these services and were to operate for 6 months when a decision would be made on the experiment continuing. A Ford Transit commercial vehicle was chosen which was modified with windows and seating by Strachans (Hamble).

Since these vehicles have a very limited life under such operating conditions, it is highly unlikely that a bus of this capacity will ever pay its way, let alone cover the direct operating costs. Apart from the Highgate Village service, the Ford was able to cope with passenger loadings and those on the C11 were replaced early in 1975 by some Bristol LHS buses with Eastern Coachworks bodies. Further buses of this type replaced the FSs on the other three routes in 1977.

A little more success was attached to the Dial-a-Bus service operated in the Golders Green area by Finchley (FY). 3 buses were allocated to this service which started late 1974. Passengers were able to phone to be picked up on a previously declared system of routes between Golders Green and Hampstead at a fare of 15p. To all intents and purposes this was very popular, but the service is unsuitable for anything bigger than this mini-bus.

The Dial-a-bus service has been discontinued and the 3 vehicles transferred to Route H2, retaining the 3 FS vehicles on a circular service between the Dial-a-bus terminals.

A new service PB1 has been introduced with the Local Authority at Potters Bar utilising 1 FS and 1 spare from the existing 21 vehicles.

These 5 FS type vehicles are to be replaced by a type yet to be decided.

(*Below*) Ford minibus with Strachan conversion body for routes with low traffic demand.

Chassis details MAKER'S REF: LC 17 TRANSIT

Track	Front 5′ 5½″, rear 5′ 1½″
Overall length	16′ 10″
Wheelbase	9′ 10″
Front axle	Leaf springs with telescopic shock absorbers
Rear axle	Leaf spring with telescopic shock absorbers
Clutch	Dry plate
Engine	Ford 2·2 litre diesel
Suspension	Leaf springs
Brakes	Vacuum servo/hydraulics
Swept circle	40′ 10″

Body details

Overall height	8′ 9¾″ (Unladen)	*Unladen weight*	2 tons 2 cwt.
Overall width	7′ 0¼″	*Laden weight*	3 tons 3 cwt.
Seating	16		
Angle of tilt	35·5°		

Vehicles built

FS 1–17   Strachan body (Mini Buses)
   18–20   Strachan body (Dial-a-bus)
      21   Dormobile (additional vehicle)

(*Below*) Production single-deck Metro-Scania, MS4.

163

60 MS Type 1973

ALTHOUGH by 1973 the decision was to use double-deckers where they could be operated, it was known that M.C.W., in conjunction with Scania Vabis, were to introduce a double-deck-version of the current single-decker which L.T. had used at Plumstead earlier. Since the running units were to be identical and L.T. were interested in an alternative up-to-date double-decker, it was decided to purchase six such single-deck buses and gain early experience before making a decision on double-deck purchase.

By bus standards these vehicles were of a high standard of comfort. Air suspension was used on both axles, the rear suspension being in the form of a sub-frame supported at the four corners by air bags. For the front axle a rigid beam was used but with air bags replacing the conventional leaf spring. A transverse engine was fitted at the rear, coupled to which is a torque convertor and thence by angled drive to the rear axle.

By suitable noise insulation built into the body and by employing two engine coolant radiators, it was found possible to achieve an all-time low noise level of 76dba.

Partly because of the air suspension and the need for an air compressor, the brakes are naturally air. A new feature to L.T. was the use of spring brakes, which come into operation automatically should the air pressure system fail. Such elaborate safety systems are not without their problems when moving a broken-down vehicle.

The six vehicles were allocated in 1973 to Dalston to operate Route S2 (formerly Route 208), beside the Leyland Nationals. Although popular with the staff, the provision of a torque converter is not without a penalty in fuel consumption.

164 double-deck Metropolitan (MD as they are known) were delivered in 1976/77 for operation from Peckham and New Cross garages.

Chassis details MAKER'S REF: METRO SCANIA

Track	Front 6′ 11″, rear 6′ 1″
Overall length	33′ 9 7/16″
Wheelbase	17′ 0 11/16″
Frame	Independent rear sub-frame
Front axle	I section beam forging
Rear axle	Spiral bevel 5·13 ratio opposed taper rollers
Gearbox	Scania HR 501 fully-automatic torque convertor
Engine	Scania D 11 oil engine 190 bhp at 2200 rpm
Suspension	Full-air rolling-lobe bellows
Brakes	Split air system spring brakes
Swept circle	64′ 4″
Steering	Power-assisted ZF type

Body details

Overall height 9′ 5″

Overall width 8′ 2½″

Passengers
Seated 37, standing 29

Unladen weight   8 tons 12 cwt.

61 LS Type 1973

Before 1973, British Leyland had carried out a survey on the future requirements of the Bus Industry in respect of vehicles. From this it was deduced that future vehicles would be single-deck with a small proportion of double-deck. Accordingly, in conjunction with the National Bus Co., a joint manufacturing company was set up to manufacture the Leyland National at Workington.

London Transport had by this time redeclared its faith in the double-decker but nevertheless there were one or two points in the National which were of interest and might be applied, should Leyland ever design a double-decker as a 'National' vehicle. Accordingly, six vehicles were ordered to complete Route S2 as well as the Metro Scanias already ordered.

The six vehicles were built on the production line at Workington and then taken to Leyland where the new close-ratio 5-speed gearbox and charged coupling were fitted. This was thought to be the transmission of the future with the exception that it should be hydraulically-actuated and not air as at present. As the engine is the relatively small 500 engine turbo-charged instead of the well-proven 0680 derated, L.T. were anxious to observe the behaviour of the engine on initial acceleration and life expectancy.

The vehicles were still in service as this book goes to press. A further 51 vehicles have been supplied to enable the SM vehicles to be withdrawn from Hounslow (AV). It is also intended to bring the original six generally more in line with the 51 and work all 57 from Hounslow. An additional 50 buses are now being delivered, commencing at Elmers End, to replace SM vehicles.

A decision has now been taken to withdraw all SM/SMS vehicles and authority has been given to purchase up to another 160 vehicles.

(*Below*) The first Leyland National bus built for London Transport: LS1.

Chassis details MAKER'S REF: 1051/2R

Track	Front 6′ 10″, rear 6′ 1″
Overall length	33′ 10$\frac{13}{16}$″
Wheelbase	16′ 7$\frac{13}{16}$″
Frame	Front and rear sub-frames
Front axle	Reversed Elliot beam with taper roller bearings
Rear axle	5·68:1 double reduction spiral bevel
Gearbox	5 speed close ratio air-operated
Clutch	Fully charged fluid coupling
Engine	Leyland 510 supercharged 4·65″ bore × 4·92″ stroke 180 bhp at 2000 rpm
Suspension	Full air with rolling diaphragm bellows
Brakes	Split-air-braking system spring brake
Swept circle	65′ 4″
Steering	Rack-and-pinion with hydraulic assistance

Body details

Overall height	10′ 8″	*Unladen weight*	8 tons 13 cwt.
Overall width	8′ 2½″	*Laden weight*	13 tons 3 cwt.
Passengers	seated 36, standing 29		

Vehicles built

LS 1–6   Leyland (Workington) body series I
  7–57   Leyland (Workington) body series II
 58–107   Leyland (Workington) body series II (minor body modifications)

62 OM Type

THESE VEHICLES, although operated by London Transport for the Round London Sight-seeing Tour are, in fact, owned by Obsolete Fleet and are on hire, even though painted in L.T. livery.

The vehicles are ex Birmingham and Midland Motor Omnibus Co's D9 design and were taken over at the time the West Midlands Passenger Transport Excutive purchased the Birmingham City Services. These vehicles were surplus to requirements and were sold.

The covered tops were removed by 'L.P.C. Hounslow' and small-depth windows were fitted along the upper deck to maintain a safety height. The front and rear bulkhead windows were left to give a windbreak.

The vehicles were given bonnet letters OM and were operated from the 1975 season and are currently operated by Stockwell garage (SW).

Chassis details MAKER'S REF: MIDLAND RED D9

Overall length	30′
Frame	Integral chassisless construction
Front axle	Not fitted as front wheels are independently carried
Rear axle	Fully floating worm drive axle 5·5:1
Gearbox	S.C.G. RV 35 oil-operated planetary 4 speed electrically selected
Clutch	Fluid clutch (fluid flywheel with centrifugal clutch)
Engine	B.M.M.O. 10·5 litre 124 mm. bore × 145 mm. stroke 6 cylinder oil engine
Suspension	Metalastik individual trailing arms front. Metalastik toggle links for rear axle.
Brakes	Originally disc front converted to drum rear wheels drum. Continuous flow hydraulic
Steering	Marles cam-and-double-roller, with power assistance 28·5:1

Body details

Overall width 8′   *Seating* 72

63 BS Type 1975

ON ONE of the Mini-bus routes (C11) it was found that the seating capacity of the Ford FS was insufficient for the traffic and, furthermore, the duty was rather arduous for this type of lightweight vehicle.

A market survey indicated that the only vehicle that met the requirements was probably the short wheelbase Bristol LH (more usually designated LHS). As the need for these was urgent, they had to be purchased without modification to suit L.T. requirements.

All six purchased were fitted with an E.C.W. standard 26-seater body. Later in 1976 a further 11 were purchased, again to a standard specification, but being fitted with a more suitable 4-speed gearbox, which allowed all the FS buses to be withdrawn from the original routes.

(*Left*) The Midland Red bus, (OM1), after conversion to open top for the Round London Sightseeing Tour.

Chassis details MAKER'S REF: BRISTOL LHS

Track	Front 6′ 5″, rear 5′ 8⅝″
Overall length	24′ 0″
Wheelbase	12′ 6″
Frame	Pressed steel 8″ deep channel
Front axle	I section beam adjustable taper roller bearings
Rear axle	Fully floating 5·57:1 ratio single spiral bevel drive taper roller bearings
Gearbox	5 speed heavy duty synchromesh Turner/Clarke T5/400 (Synchro 2, 3, 4 and
(For BS 1-6).	5th).
Clutch	Borg-&-Beck single dry-plate AS15
Engine	Leyland 0·401 6 cylinder oil 125 bhp at 2400 rpm
Suspension	Semi-elliptical leaf-spring shock absorbers, front and rear
Brakes	Dual circuit air pressure drum brakes wedge operated
Swept circle	43′
Steering	Burman recirculating ball with 32·5:1 ratio

Body details

Overall height	9′ 9½″	*Unladen weight*	5 tons 8 cwt.
Overall width	7′ 6½″	*Laden weight*	7 tons 2 cwt.
Seating	26		
Angle of tilt	36°		

Vehicles built

BS 1–17 E.C.W. body

(*Below*) Bristol LHS bus for the C11 Holloway service.

64 BL Type 1975

The RF vehicle was first introduced in1952 and its replacement was originally arranged to be the MB and later SM. When the licensing authorities indicated that on certain routes they were no longer prepared to accept vehicles any wider than 7′ 6″, it became imperative to find a replacement. Of only two alternatives, the Bristol LH was chosen and certain features were built in to suit L.T. These included power steering, automatic brake adjustment, fluid transmission and revised pedal arrangement to give a better ergonomic arrangement.

Delivery of these 95 vehicles began at the end of 1975.

Chassis details MAKER'S REF: BRISTOL LH

Track	Front 6′ 5″, rear 5′ 8½″	*Overall length*	30, 1″
Wheelbase	16′ 2″	*Frame*	Pressed steel 8″ deep channel
Front axle	I section beam adjustable taper roller bearings		
Rear axle	Fully floating 5·57:1 ratio single spiral bevel differential taper roller bearings		
Gearbox	Bristol/S.C.G. direct acting epicyclic		
Clutch	18″ fluid flywheel		
Engine	Leyland 0·401 engine 6 cylinder oil 125 bhp at 2400 rpm		
Suspension	Leaf-spring semi-elliptic shock absorbers, front and rear		
Brakes	Dual-circuit air-pressure drum brakes, with spring parking brake at rear.		
Steering	Power-assisted Burman recirculating ball 25·2:1 ratio		

Body details

Overall height	10′ 0″	*Unladen weight*	5 tons 14 cwt.
Overall width	7′ 6″	*Laden weight*	8 tons 9 cwt.
Seating	39		

Vehicles built

BL 1–95 E.C.W. body

Note: BL93, 94 and 95 have been purchased by Hillingdon Borough Council for operation of new route 128 by LT.. The lighter relief is coloured yellow.

(*Below*) Bristol LH single-decker: BL36.

65 **B15 Type** 1976

THESE PROTOTYPE double-deck vehicles were designed to meet the new environmental requirements of reducing noise levels. At the same time the design was seen as the next generation of double-deckers.

Before this time market research had indicated that future buses would be of the single-deck design and, based on this, Leyland in conjunction with National Bus, had set up the Workington factory to produce a standard 'National' single-deck bus, as outlined in earlier chapters.

Some of the major operators, including London Transport, found that their large single-deckers were unmanageable in City Centres, and operators purchased double-deckers. As one-man operation was a basic requirement, the only real choice of vehicle was between the Leyland Atlantean and Daimler Fleetline.

The return to leaf springs suspension for a future generation of buses was totally unacceptable to many operators and with legislation affecting environmental noise, Leyland set about designing an up-to-date double-deck bus for the 1980s.

Co-operation was sought from various major operators, including L.T., as it was intended to produce a vehicle with world-wide sales appeal rather than just for a particular operator. It is for this reason that this vehicle contains certain features which would not necessarily be included if it were being designed specifically for L.T.

In order to assist Leyland in its testing of B15, L.T. agreed to test one vehicle initially on Route 24 followed by a period on Route 16. It is envisaged that the test would last

(*Below*) Prototype B15.

170

about 18 months during which time the vehicle will be evaluated from all aspects. Production will then commence. The test (1st stage) was completed on Route 24 and the vehicle returned to Leyland for exhibition at the 1976 Commercial Motor Show.

The design incorporates an independent front suspension with torsion bar control for the unladen weight but incorporating air suspension bellows for the passenger weight. Rear suspension is by bogie frame with air bellows at each corner giving consistent height control.

Transmission is by charged coupling and 5-speed close ratio 'hydracyclic' epicyclic gearbox, with automatic gear control. The engine is mounted transverse at the rear and is of the Leyland 500 type, incorporating a fixed head i.e., no detachable cylinder heads. In order to keep pollution to a minimum, turbo-charging is used adding also to the general quietness.

Braking is very similar to that employed on the Routemaster with the addition of a spring parking brake.

To add to passenger comfort, a relatively low flat floor-line has been used at the expense, in some cases, of the location of mechanical components.

The outcome of the extensive test programme in London service and its influence on the production design of B15 is awaited with interest.

Chassis details MAKER'S REF: B15

Overall length	31′ 4⅝″
Wheelbase	16′ 6″
Front axle	Independently supported king post assemblies
Rear axle	Double reduction drop centre 4·974:1 ratio with angle drive 1·04:1
Gearbox	5 speed close ratio with G2 automatic control—electro-hydraulic operation
Clutch	Charged coupling
Engine	Leyland 501 fixed-head turbo-charged 6 cylinder oil 170 bhp at 2000 rpm *
Suspension	Front:– independent torsion bars coupled with air
	Rear:– Self-levelling H frame with air suspension
Brakes	Lockheed continuous flow, hydraulic power
Swept circle	64′ 8½″
Steering	Powered rack-and-pinion

* Note: Gardner 6LXB now being offered

Body details

Overall height 14′ 5⅛″   *Overall width* 8′ 2½″   *Seating:* Inside 27; Outside 44

---

66 MD Type 1976

WITH THE CHANGEOVER of production of the Daimler Fleetline chassis from Coventry to Leyland, difficulties arose in meeting L.T.'s order. Double-deck vehicles were urgently required to replace the ageing RT, and also to enable MB vehicles to be withdrawn, an order was placed with M.C.W. for the supply of 164 Metropolitans, all-metal welded construction bodies fitted with Scania mechanical running units.

These 164 are similar in mechanical ways to the six single-deck Scanias (MS Chapter 60) but advantage has been taken to improve the fuel consumption by introducing a lower lock-up speed for direct drive on the torque converter.

All the vehicles are scheduled to be allocated to Peckham and New Cross garages, starting initially with the 36 and 63 group of routes, and subsequently Route 53.

Chassis details MAKER'S REF: METROPOLITAN

Track	Front 6′ 11½″, rear 6′ 0½″
Overall length	31′ 10″
Wheelbase	16′ 10″
Frame	Independent rear sub-frame
Front axle	I section beam forging
Rear axle	Spiral bevel 5·57 ratio opposed taper roller bearings
Gearbox *Clutch*	} Scania fully automatic torque convertor
Engine	Scania D11002 6 cylinder oil engine 190 bhp at 2200 rpm
Suspension	Air rolling lobe bellows
Brakes	Split air system with spring brakes
Swept circle	64′
Steering	Power assisted ZF type

Body details

Overall height	14′ 5½″	*Overall width* 8′ 2½″	
Seating	inside 27, outside 43	*Angle of tilt* 28°	

Vehicles built

MD1–164   M.C.W. all metal body

(*Below*) The first Metropolitan bus: MD1.

(*Above*) The special bus for the Round London Sightseeing Tour. Seven Daimler Fleetlines were bought from Bournemouth Corporation during 1977. The roof is detachable and the buses will replace the OM vehicles for use on the Tour run by London Transport every day, throughout the year. Mechanically, the buses are similiar to the XF class, without power steering; they have little family comparison with the DMS type.

Appendix 1 **Central Area Garages**

The list includes all garages which have operated buses
Garages such as Isleworth (IH) closed on trolleybus conversion have been omitted.

	Code	First date of operation	
Abbey Wood	AW		Former tram/trolleybus depot
Alperton	ON	1939	
Athol St.	C	1907	Closed 1961
Barking	BK	1924	
Battersea	B	1906	
Bexley	BX	1935	Former trolleybus depot
Bow	BW	1908	Former tram/trolleybus depot
Brixton	BN	1903	Former tram depot
Brixton Private Hire	BT	1927	Ex Cambrian Landray. Closed 1938
Bromley	TB	1924	Used by Thomas Tilling buses until 1933
Camberwell	Q	1914	
Camden Town	AQ	1912	Ex British. Closed 1933
Carshalton	CN	1906	Former tram/trolleybus depot
Catford	TL	1914	Used by Thomas Tilling buses in 1920-1933
Chalk Farm	CF	1916	
Chelverton Rd.	AF	1912	Renamed Putney in 1958
Chiswick BEA	–		Former tram depot
Clapham	CA	1906	Former tram depot. Closed 1958, later became Museum
Clapton	CT	1909	Former tram/trolleybus depot
Clay Hall	CL	1931	Closed 1959
Crayford	CR	1917	Handed over to East Surrey 1931
Cricklewood	W	1905	
Croydon	TC	1916	Used by Thomas Tilling buses until 1933
Dalston	D	1907	
East Ham	EH	1926	Ex Atlas/Invicta. Closed 1931
Edgware	EW	1925	Rebuilt 1939
Edmonton	EM	1905	Former tram/trolleybus depot
Elmers End	ED	1929	
Enfield	E	1928	Ex Public (code first used for Acton closed 1925)
Farm Lane	F	1906	Closed 1914
Finchley	FY	1905	Former tram/trolleybus depot
Forest Gate	G	1911	Ex Great Eastern closed 1960
Fulwell	FW	1902	Former tram/trolleybus depot
Hackney	H	1911	
Hammersmith	HB	1908	Former tram/trolleybus depot then B.E.A. Closed
Hanwell	HL	1901	Former tram/trolleybus depot
Harrow Weald	HD	1930	
Hendon	AE	1913	
Highgate	HT	1908	Former tram/trolleybus depot—renamed Holloway in 1971
Holloway	J	1911	Closed 1971
Hornchurch	RD	1924	Known as Romford until 1935
Hounslow	AV	1913	
Kingston	K	1922	(code first used for Kilburn closed 1915)
Leyton	T	1912	
Loughton	L	1923	

Merton	AL	1913	
Middle Row	X	1910	
Mortlake	M	1906	
Muswell Hill	MH	1925	
New Cross	NX	1906	Former tram depot
Norbiton	NB	1952	
North St. Romford	NS	1952	
Norwood	N	1909	
Nunhead	AH	1910	Ex National Steam Car. Closed 1954
Old Kent Rd.	P	1908	Closed 1958
Palmers Green	AD	1912	
Peckham	PM	1951	
Plumstead	AM	1913	
Poplar	PR	1906	Former tram/trolleybus depot
Potters Bar	PB	1930	Used by Overground buses until 1933
Putney Bridge	F	1913	Ex National Steam Car. Closed 1958 (code first used for Farm Lane closed 1914)
Riverside	R	1913	Known as Hammersmith until 1950
Rye Lane	RL	1951	Closed 1969
Seven Kings	AP	1913	
Shepherd's Bush	S	1908	
Sidcup	SP	1924	
Southall	HW	1925	Known as Hanwell until 1950
South Harrow	SH	1925	Dormy shed closed 1930
Stamford Hill	SF	1906	Former tram/trolleybus depot
Stockwell	SW	1952	
Stonebridge	SE	1906	Former tram/trolleybus depot
Streatham	AK	1913	
Sutton	A	1924	(Code first used for Albany St. Closed 1916)
Thornton Heath	TH	1901	Former tram depot
Tottenham	AR	1913	
Turnham Green	V	1911	
Twickenham	AB	1912	Closed 1970
Upton Park	U	1907	Rebuilt 1930
Uxbridge	UX	1922	Used by Thames Valley 1922–29
Victoria	GM	1940	
Walworth	WL	1905	Former tram depot
Walthamstow	WW	1905	Former tram/trolleybus depot
Wandsworth	WD	1905	Former tram/trolleybus depot
West Green	WG	1925	Ex Public. Closed 1962
West Ham	WH	1906	Former tram/trolleybus depot
Weybridge	WB	1923	Dormy shed closed 1939
Willesden	AC	1912	
Wood Green	WN	1904	Former tram/trolleybus depot

Appendix 2 Country Area Garages

Listed from 1933 until vesting day (London Country) January 1970

Addelstone	WY	1936	
Amersham	MA	1935	
Bishop's Stortford	BS		Closed 1934
Chelsham	CM	1925	
Crawley	CY	1928	
Crayford	CR	1917	Closed 1933
Dartford	DT	1926	Ex Maidstone & District
Dorking	DS	1931	
Dunton Green	DG	1922	
East Grinstead	EG	1925	
Epping	EP	1934	Closed 1963
Garston	GR	1952	
Godstone	GD	1925	
Grays	GY	1935	
Guildford	GF	1930	
Harlow	HA	1963	
Hatfield	HF	1922	Rebuilt 1958/9
Hemel Hempstead	HH	1935	
Hertford	HG	1935	
High Wycombe	HE	1928	Closed 1977
Hitchin	HN		Closed 1959
Leatherhead	LH	1925	
Luton	LS	1920	Purchased from Strawhatter 1933. Closed 1976
Northfleet	NF	1936	
Reigate	RG	1932	
Romford (London Rd.)	RE	1923	Ex Hillman. Closed
Slough, Alpha St	SL	1926	Closed 1933
Slough, Bath Rd	SU	1930	Ex Premier Line. Closed 1936
St. Albans	SA	1936	
Staines	ST	1930	
Stevenage	SV	1959	
Swanley	SJ	1923	
Tring	TG	1935	Closed 1977
Tunbridge Wells	TW	1922	Closed 1966
Watford High St.	WA		Closed 1952
Watford Leavesden Rd.	WT	1920	Closed 1952
Windsor	WR	1932	

Appendix 3 **Long-term hired vehicles**

(*Above*) Daimler on long-term hire from Maidstone Corporation. It is shown here at Sutton Garage.

(*Left*) Southend Corporation PD3 on extended loan in 1976.

Appendix 4 **Vehicles of Interest**

(*Above*) Experimental A.E.C. double-decker with forward engine mounted beneath cab. This Regent Mark IV never ran in service.

W. J. Haynes

(*Below*) Three-axle coach purchased from Sampsons of Cheshunt; this Bedford VAL with Plaxton body is in use for development work on future bus designs.